The EDCF Guide to Digital Cinema Production

The EDCF
Guide to Digital Cinema Production

Edited by

Lasse Svanberg

ELSEVIER

AMSTERDAM • BOSTON • HEIDELBERG • LONDON
NEW YORK • OXFORD • PARIS • SAN DIEGO
SAN FRANCISCO • SINGAPORE • SYDNEY • TOKYO

Focal Press is an imprint of Elsevier

Focal Press is an imprint of Elsevier
200 Wheeler Road, Burlington, MA 01803, USA
Linacre House, Jordan Hill, Oxford OX2 8DP, UK

Recognizing the importance of preserving what has been written, Elsevier prints its books on acid-free paper whenever possible.

Library of Congress Cataloging-in-Publication Data
Application submitted.

British Library Cataloging-in-Publication Data
A catalogue record for this book is available from the British Library.

ISBN: 0-240-80663-8

For information on all Focal Press publications
visit our website at www.focalpress.com

04 05 06 07 08 09   10 9   8 7 6 5 4 3 2 1

Printed in the United States of America

Contents

Foreword

European Digital Cinema Forum is proud to present this *Guide to Digital Film Production*. EDCF was constituted three years ago, more specifically in Stockholm on 13 June 2001. Sweden's EU Presidency offered a well-timed opportunity to launch a European E- and D-cinema initiative, since we at that time had developed a good working relationship with our counterparts in Great Britain and France, based on cooperation and trust.

Our joint ambition was to create a European network for all those who wanted to participate actively in the development of digital cinema in Europe. One thing was for sure at that time: the digital evolution would bring with it radical changes in all parts of European cinema – in production, exhibition, content, industrial structures and business models. In all these areas we should expect increased diversity.

The digital breakthrough has not yet occurred, that's true. During the past three years of activity EDCF has, however, experienced a change of mood, from scepticism (and in some cases aggression) to a general recognition that digital cinema is definitely coming; the question is just *when* and *how?*

Post-production is all digital by now. In Sweden and Denmark half of all feature films made are today being produced on digital media. All around Europe various projects are testing out technology and content for digital film exhibition. This usually occurs within the framework of cultural policies and co-financed by public support. Digital cinema opens unique possibilities for decentralized distribution of a more diversified repertoire of films and other audiovisual content, in accordance with the needs of European filmmakers and audiences. The commercial cinema industry has, however, been restrained by insecurity around technical standard issues, high levels of technical investments and structural challenges, which has prevented a large-scale and commercially well-founded roll out of digital cinema.

It has for long been evident that a breakthrough for European Digital Cinema is very dependent on strategic decisions taken in Hollywood: 'Without standards, no business.' For that reason, EDCF decided, from day one, to establish itself as the self-evident European discussion partner for the American film industry (see Chapter 8, 'Standards'). We are very glad that we succeeded in this ambition and have created a constructive transatlantic dialogue which today, three years after the birth of EDCF, means that we can anticipate reasonable global standard recommendations for digital cinema by the end of 2004.

Technological breakthroughs have, historically, not only made it possible for us to produce things cheaper, faster and better, they have also added new work methods and entirely new ways of expression. This certainly applies to present times when cinema is about to go digital. Filmmakers are closely tied to and dependent on their technical work tools. The ongoing change from analogue to digital requires new knowledge and new ways of thinking, in order to fully exploit the potentials of the new medium. While the mechanical tradition founded hierarchies, digital technology creates networks.

The European film landscape has traditionally been almost hopelessly fragmented, due to national borders, different languages, religions and cultures. These differences have partly been hailed in the name of 'cultural diversity' but have also weakened European cinema in relation to the strong and well coordinated American film industry.

The development of the European Union, in combination with the techno-economical convergences which today's digital technology facilitates, should be seen as a threat to 'old bastions' and therefore requires the creation of sustainable and innovative new networks in Europe. It is my and EDCF's sincere hope that this book will contribute to such a development within the production community and furthermore speed up an intelligent, broad-minded, culturally and commercially sound implementation of digital cinema in Europe and elsewhere.

Special thanks are due to the Editor of this book, professor Lasse Svanberg, who for many years has been a critical but at the same time constructive power centre in the Nordic film and media debate.

Åse Kleveland
Chair EDCF, CEO Swedish Film Institute

Preface

This book is intended as a practical and hands-on look at the process of HD film production for both students and working professionals in the film industry and furthermore a basis for discussions on how the transition from analogue to digital technology can be accomplished in the best possible ways.

Since the very early days of humanity, we have shared an urge to tell stories to explain who we are and what we feel. The tools for storytelling have evolved from sharp rocks to colour paints, from skin canvases to written words, from hand-crafted books to mass-printed newspapers to eventually moving images, movies and television. Now we are on the threshold of an even more exciting era, the era of digital cinema, which promises to deliver a higher quality cinema experience to future movie enthusiasts.

A lot has changed and a lot will change in the film production process as it slowly but surely transforms itself from an analogue, mechanical and celluloid one into a digital, programmed and electronic one. For most, this change is a positive and exciting one, as it lets the filmmaker's imagination jump in leaps and bounds into fantastic new worlds. For some, this change is seen as a threat and a decisive turn to qualities that do not represent the best that filmmaking can offer. The aim of this guide is to give a timely overview on the state of the industry through case studies, to answer questions that are most often raised about digital cinema and to further the dialogue among professionals about the best practices in digital film production.

This book was born through the vision of the EDCF and especially its dynamic chairwoman, Åse Kleveland, and would not have been realized without the experience and patience of Editor Lasse Svanberg.

The pre-print phase of this book has been financed by generous grants from the Finnish Ministry of Education, the Swedish Film Institute and with the valuable cooperation of the Centre of Cultural Expertise in Helsinki, Culminatum Ltd. We are grateful that Focal Press, the leading publisher of international books on the development of moving picture technology, has taken this book project on board and given it the added benefit of its solid publishing experience.

Johannes Lassila
Chair, EDCF Content Module
Producer, Perfecto Films, Helsinki

1

Why Digital?

Introduction

Lasse Svanberg

The cinema – storytelling in a flow of consecutive images which meet in secret, poetic under-standing – is an ancient artform, the celluloid film strip just its latest technical phase. Latest, not last. We will soon be filming without film and without tapes.

(Swedish film critic Bengt Idestam-Almquist, *When Cinema Came to Sweden*, published 1959)

This quotation is 45 years old, published at a time when the first 2 inch VTRs were introduced, revolutionizing the way television was made and transmitted. Yet – with incredible foresight – these few lines describe exactly where we are today. More and more feature films are being shot not on film, but on digital video media. At the same time videotape is beginning to disappear as a recording medium in the television industry (at least in news gathering), being gradually replaced by faster and more cost-effective hard disc and solid state solutions. And our need for 'storytelling in a flow of consecutive images which meet in secret, poetic understanding' is greater than ever before.

I recently retired from the Swedish Film Institute after 34 years of public service as 'tech scout', meaning that it was my responsibility to look ahead and inform others – through seminars and '*Technology & Man Magazine*' (*Teknik och Människa, T&M*) – of what could be reasonably expected from technical developments in the near future, in terms of new work tools, methods and ideas for the production of moving images.

Nobody knows (or can know) with certainty on which media we will be shooting moving images 20 or even 10 years from now. The techno-cycles are getting shorter and shorter in the Digital Age, the lifetime of recording systems, standards and work procedures is being reduced. Let me therefore start by looking back. As Swedish poet Alf Henriksson said: 'In order to know where we are going, we have to know where we have been.'

The History

'The Digital Age', how often have you heard this phrase during the past decade? When did it start? (And when will it end?) Most people seem to associate the Digital Age concept with the global breakthrough of the Internet and the World Wide Web (1995–2000) – the fastest breakthrough in the history of technical innovations. The film and TV industry, however, started its process of 'digitalization' when the first microcomputers arrived in the early 1980s, initially used for process control in film labs, lighting control in film studios and automatic control of animation cameras. Digital audio was introduced in the mid-1980s and the first digital VTR in 1989. LucasFilm presented its revolutionary EditDroid and SoundDroid in 1983. The first half of the 1990s brought with it an avalanche of technical innovation and radical changes in the form of (among others) digital offline non-linear editing and digital special effects, the latter creating digital SFX 'factories' in California which mass produced space monsters, intergalactic mass destruction, man-eating dinosaurs, earthquakes, tornados, fires and other natural catastrophes in a previously unseen image quality and quantity.

Film is Dead!

Cinematographic film has been declared dead many times in history, both as a recording and distribution medium. First, when television was introduced in the early 1950s. Why go to the movies when you can see moving pictures in your own living room – for free (in the United States)! Then when portable professional VTRs became available. Why shoot on film when you can shoot on videotape and immediately see what you have recorded?

In 1972 I went to Hollywood to make a special issue of *T&M Magazine* on 'Video Film' (that was at the time when Vidtronics were big on videotape-to-film transfers). I met, among others, the legendary Director of Photography Lee Garmes (one of the DoPs on *Gone With the Wind*), who had just finished shooting his first feature on videotape, *Why?* (a suitable title since film transfers looked pretty bad at that time). Garmes stated, without hesitation: 'I hope I will never see a piece of film again.'

'Film is dead!' was cried out even louder when home video hit the market in a big way in the early 1980s. Why go to the movies when you can rent VHS cassettes of all new films, for less than the price of a cinema ticket and in a gas station or videoshop near you? Yes, it killed large numbers of smaller cinemas in suburbs and in the rural communities, but the cinema industry as a whole prevailed.

When the Japanese launched analogue HDTV in the late 1980s, American director Francis F. Coppola became so enthusiastic over the

HDTV-to-film transfers he saw in Tokyo that he went home to San Francisco and created an all-electronic film production system named SLEK (So Long Eastman Kodak). His company went bust while Eastman Kodak still thrives (although eagerly diversifying into the digital domain). The HDTV-to-film transfers, however, looked quite good, good enough to make raw stock manufacturers a bit worried. HDTV was, however, analogue at that time, which turned out to be a *very* expensive cul-de-sac for the Japanese and European electronics industry, and it took almost 10 years before a somewhat sustainable digital HDTV alternative was presented as a feature film recording medium. Sony and Matsushita bought a major part of the Hollywood studios (Columbia and Universal) in the mid-1990s and 'hard-sold' HDTV-based film production techniques to Hollywood filmmakers. Unsuccessfully. It was only George Lucas who at that time did not want to see a piece of film again.

Why then has a 'stone age' technology like the photo-chemical film process managed to survive all these attacks from the electronics industry?

- Film has, for more than one hundred years, been a well-established *world standard* both in production, distribution and exhibition (and there are no real world standards in the world of electronics).
- Film history has also set the standards for screen-writing, storytelling techniques and dramaturgy.
- Cinema film is still the waterhole that attracts the biggest creative buffalos (and a few hyenas), because of its superior audiovisual impact (the large screen, the captive audience) plus the international glamour and artistic prestige which still characterizes the elite in the film industry, both on national and international levels.
- Cinematographic film still holds the lead as a recording medium in terms of *resolution power* and is furthermore far superior as a medium for long term archiving with its guaranteed lifetime of up to 500 years (properly stored).

'The Incredible Shrinking Game'

The technical developments during the past two decades have meant tremendous improvements in information packaging density and in reduction of the size of equipment. It is clearly visible in Fig. 1.1*A*, showing the area (in square millimetres) which one second of images and sound occupy on different information carriers, from 35 mm film and 2 inch videotape to 6 mm mini-DV videotape.

The reduction of equipment size, price and manning requirements have been especially dramatic in the television industry, as Table 1.1 and Fig. 1.1*B*

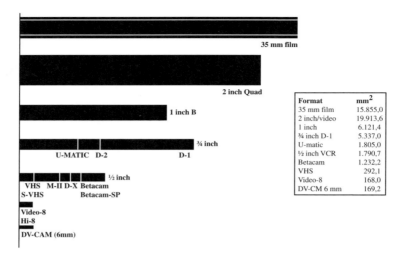

Format	mm^2
35 mm film	15.855,0
2 inch/video	19.913,6
1 inch	6.121,4
¾ inch D-1	5.337,0
U-matic	1.805,0
½ inch VCR	1.790,7
Betacam	1.232,2
VHS	292,1
Video-8	168,0
DV-CM 6 mm	169,2

Fig 1.1 Area required (in mm^2) to carry one second of images in different video formats and 35 mm film (Copyright *T&M Magazine* 1998; reproduced with permission).

(an almost outrageous simplification of a very complicated and 35-year-long process) show.

Let us hope the future does not hold 0.5 man teams (although it would be considered progress by broadcast TV economists). For someone like me, who shot my first feature film in 1966 with a blimped Arriflex 35 mm camera (weighing some 20 kilos) it is actually 'mind-blowing' that you can today record images and sound of broadcast quality (even acceptable on the big cinema screen) with a camera that almost fits into your jacket

Table 1.1 Approximate weight of equipment, minimum manning requirements and price of equipment for the acquisition of location shots in broadcast quality

Year	Format	Weight (kg)	Manning	Price (Euro)*
1960	2 inch videotape	200	10	300 000
1975	³/4-inch videotape	20 (back-pack)	4	40 000
1995	¹/2-inch Beta tape	10	2	30 000
2004	¹/4-inch (6 mm) DV tape	0.5	1	3 000

*Ball-park figures.

pocket, costs no more than 3000 Euro and has built-in 'Steadicam'. I am quite surprised that this new possibility has not changed the structure of the big broadcast TV dinosaurs more than it has. Powers of inertia, I would guess; or the old German saying at work, 'Why make it simple, when it can be made so *wonderfully* complicated!'

When it comes to digital feature film production do not forget that a fully equipped and film-styled HD (high definition) video camera is just as bulky as a blimped 35 mm film camera, even bulkier if you count in the large HD monitor in the package. HD camcorders will, however, decrease in size and weight in the near future.

Silver or Rust?

The 'video vs. film' debate accelerated in the early 1990s. In 1995 I received an SMPTE award and the ceremony was preceded by a presentation by Lawrence Thorpe, a very powerful speaker, on Sony's latest video camera marvel and its merits as a new filmmaking tool. Since I was the first award recipient I could not resist the temptation of turning to him (at the end of my acceptance speech) and observing that 'fifteen years of experience as a DoP tells me that the really important thing is not what you've got *in* the camera – film or video, silver or rust – the important things is what you've got *in front of* and *behind* the camera'. This was followed by a dead silence and I asked myself, what have I said? Then one person started to applaud and another joined in, out of a crowd of some two hundred (probably the only two DoPs present!).

I still haven't figured out if the silence was an expression of disapproval or total lack of understanding. A brutally simple conclusion would be that motion picture and television engineers (mostly grey-haired men) have no interest in what happens in front of and behind the camera, they are only interested in the camera itself and the engineering beauty in the technical parameters of the recording system connected to it. Why otherwise would the electronic 'film style' cameras that appeared at the end of the 1990s have looked the way they did?

Silver or rust? I have seen dozens of comparisons between film and video as production media, most of them biased on the silver or rust side. One of the most thorough, by Peter Swinson, appeared in the February 2004 issue of the British *Image Technology* magazine (BKSTS), comparing 35 mm, Super 16 mm and HD video acquisition (Figures 1.2, 1.3). I leave it to you to decide whether it is objective or not. In my opinion it is not very flattering for the video alternative, especially combined with Peter Swinson's complementary figure comparing image areas and resolution (in Ks) for film and video shooting formats.

	35 mm film acquisition	S16 mm film acquisition	Video acquisition
Resolution, relative to HD	Exceeds 4:1	Equates	Equates
Resolution limit	4096 × 3112	2048 × 1152	Fixed 1920 × 1080
Colour resolution	Full RGB	Full RGB	Full luma, limited chroma*
Dynamic range	6000:1	6000:1	300:1 to 1000:1
Subtle shading minimum	0.005% (14 bit)	0.005% (14 bit)	0.2% (8 bit digital)
Light sensitivity	Medium	Medium	High
Depth of field control	Very narrow to wide	Narrow to wide	Wide, narrow more difficult
Grain	Very very fine	Fine	Fine
Perception of image	Real world immersion	Realistic	Clean, pure. (Clinical)
Shooting speeds	Any. 0 to 500 fps	Any. 0 to 500 fps	24 or 25 or 30 fps
Shutter speeds at normal fps	1/50th to 1/500th	1/50th to 1/500th	1/50th to 1/2000th
TV studio ease of use	Reasonable	Good	Excellent
Controlled location shooting	Reasonable	Excellent	Good (cable runs a problem)
Wildlife locations, jungle etc.	Heavy, unsuitable	Light. Instant start. Ideal	Battery power limited. Delayed start
Instant playback	No*	No*	Yes
Cost of equipment	High	Low	Very high
Material costs	High	Medium	Medium to low
Archive capability	Excellent	Good	Poor (Format dependent)
	*Instant with video assist	*Instant with video assist	*Depends on camera and recorder

Fig 1.2 Silver or rust? Relative merits of film and HDTV (Copyright: Peter Swinson, 2004; reproduced with permission).

Three milestones

Before dealing with the present, I would like to point out three milestones in digital film production from the near past.

Toy Story was released in 1995 as the first film 'shot entirely in cyberspace'. It was entirely computer animated by Pixar and John Lassater. It was an eye-opener because it applied 'simulated cinematography' in a spectacular way – selective focus, motion-blur, DoP-type lighting in the scenes. It almost looked like it had been 'filmed' – but without film and film camera. Computer animated film is not a part of this book, since it is big enough

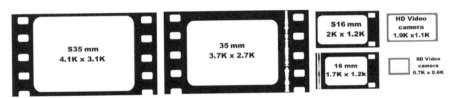

Fig 1.3 Relative image sizes of film and video formats (based on capture resolution) (Copyright: Peter Swinson, 2004; reproduced with permission).

now to require a book of its own. In the wake of what Pixar (and others) are doing today, however, lurks the biggest digital challenge of all, *The Virtual Actor* – a huge collection of 0's and 1's which looks like, sounds like and moves like a real human being.

I met John Lassater during a press conference in Stockholm in 1996 and asked him 'When can you make Humphrey Bogart?' And the answer was: 'We can make Bogey any time, but we can't make him *act* like Bogey. That's gonna take another few years.' Well, another few years have now passed. Keep in mind that Pixar (now separated from Disney) is the most lucrative film studio in California and holds bundles of creativity and R&D money.

Thomas Vinterberg's *The Celebration* ('Festen'), the first Dogma (Dogme95) movie in 1998, was shot with amateur mini-DV cameras (1-chip). Super 16 mm film and Beta video were considered as shooting formats but when the first mini-DV cameras reached the market (not long before shooting started) Vinterberg and DoP Anthony Dod Mantle decided to use them (see also 'The Danish Digital Experience' in Chapter 3). The final 35 mm blow-up resembled blow-ups of Super 8 film. The film, however, became an artistic and commercial success because of its powerful story and great acting. The success of this film sent a very important message to young filmmakers all over the world (not least in developing countries): it is quite possible to make a successful feature film with cheap Desktop Movie tools! A heavy-footed multi-million dollar machinery is *not* a prerequisite for entry to the Big Silver Screen. (The success of the American low-budget film *The Blair Witch Project* had sent similar signals and given Hollywood the shivers.)

George Lucas' *Star Wars: Episode II, The Attack of the Clones* of course played in another league – the 100 million US$ league. When principal photography started it was the first movie in the world to be shot entirely with Sony 24p HD CineAlta cameras. This *ennobled* film production without film, so to speak. LucasFilm's message to the international film industry was clear: this new way of making film should be taken *seriously!* Keep in mind that George Lucas and his Skywalker Ranch have been technical pioneers in many other areas.

There seems to be a common denominator among the directors and producers who have invested in HD video for film production at an early stage – a strong inner urge to discover unknown territory, a pioneer spirit combined with a certain contempt for the old, traditional ways of doing things. It certainly applies to George Lucas, to the Swedish, Danish and Finnish HD case studies presented in this book and to the first two HD feature films produced in France and Germany.

The Present

The present is chaos, although a creative chaos. The heavy Hollywood D-cinema tank is stuck in the Business Model mud, while the lightweight

E-cinema jeep is chugging along in Brazil, South Africa, India, China, Sweden, Holland and Great Britain, to mention a few. (For definitions of E- and D-cinema see below.) The development process of international technical standards (see Chapter 9) have led to a conflict of interests between Hollywood majors and the international cinema owner's organizations. It will be solved because it must be solved, but has, however, slowed down the work process considerably. 'Without standards, no business'.

Keep in mind that this will probably be the most complicated audiovisual standard ever presented. Note that the standard now being developed by SMPTE (the Society of Motion Picture and Television Engineers), DCI and others, in spite of its technical complexity does *not* include *production* for digital cinema since it starts at the digital cinema distribution master level. Sony's 24p HD CineAlta system became more or less a de facto HD production standard in 2000 but is expected to be replaced by RGB and 4:4:4 solutions in the near future. (At the moment of writing US director Michael Mann is, for instance, shooting major parts of his latest film, *Collateral*, with Thomson's Viper camera.)

The digital cinema concept seems to have split film pros into two camps: on the one hand the PCFs (Photo-Chemical Fundamentalists) and on the other 'digi-freaks' or neophiles who live after the motto that 'everything which is new is good, and the newest is the very best'. Analogue is old, digital is new. Both camps are represented in this book, although not in their most extreme versions.

What's the Difference between E- and D-Cinema?

One of the first missions of the EDCF was to try to lower the 'semantic noise level' and we came up with the following definitions in 2001.

- **E-cinema =** an umbrella concept embracing all forms of public electronic digital screenings of all kinds of moving pictures in cinemas or cinema-like venues.
- **D-cinema =** digital screenings of predominately new feature films in larger first-release cinemas and in a quality comparable to or better than 35 mm answer prints.
- D-cinema means traditional big-city cinemas equipped with a server and digital projector. E-cinema includes a considerable portion of non-film content (shows, concerts, sports live-events), yet still having screening of new (and classic) feature films as a main source of income. In 2001 EDCF thought that these definitions would be provisional terms and that everything would be called 'digital cinema' in the future. During 2003, however, it became clear

that the two concepts represent two different worlds (which partly overlap) and that it is still useful to make a distinction in linguistic terms.

Resolution?

The subject of resolution is the most common source of controversy today. Here we also have two camps; one which only accepts mathematical, theoretical resolution in exact numbers (measured in Ks) and another which goes by what their eyes actually see and their ears hear, in other words *experienced* resolution in a normal cinema setting. Camp 1 states that the market isn't ready because the technology isn't ready. Camp 2 claims that the technology is ready, but the market isn't. (This only applies to exhibition – the fact that HD film production technology definitely is *not* ready will appear clearly in several chapters in this book.)

In May 2002 I attended an SMPTE seminar at the Digital Cinema Laboratory (DCL) in Los Angeles. *Space Cowboys*, with an aged Clint Eastwood in the lead, was shown in its full length, as digital (from server) and as a 35 mm print – first reel digital, second reel film and so on – 19 m screen-width, 30 m throw, 1.3K projection (Christie DLP dark-chip), 8 bit colour depth. I became almost embarrassed that I, with my 'golden DoP eyes', did not notice the reel changes.

In November 2003, during a seminar at the London NFT Digital Test Bed (see Chapter 7), I listened to Bill Kinder, Manager of Post-Production at Pixar (live via satellite). We saw a trailer for their latest blockbuster, *The Incredibles*: superb screen quality in 1.3K projection. Kinder's view was that 2K is good enough for major first release cinemas for a long long time ahead, and that 1.3K is more than good enough for medium-sized cinemas, so why then Hollywood's pursuit of a 4K exhibition standard? (I understand that 4K will be important in post-production and for film archiving and restoration.) Isn't it a terrible waste of time and money, since it will make projection technology much more expensive, slow down the roll-out process considerably and make 4K digital cinemas rare and exclusive? The resolution issue is indeed controversial.

Hollywood's ambition since 2000 has been that D-cinema should show films digitally in a quality comparable to or better than 35 mm answer prints (a worthy ambition). The resolution of a 35 mm release print is generally considered to be 1.3K (in best case). 1.3K digital projection is *better than* a 35 mm release print for the simple reason that the digital image is rock-steady (no weave and jump) and has no disturbing and typical film artefacts like scratches and dirt.

We all await the outcome when SMPTE, DCI et al. present their final draft standards recommendation at the end of 2004.

Who Runs the Digital Show?

There is an academically established model for technology innovation called the PIP model – Push – Inertia – Pull. Push powers are generally of techno-economical (and therefore political) character and their main ambition is to change the social order in such a way that it promotes their own interests. Powers of inertia, stalling powers, are often of religious or political nature but the most common and least discussed part of them is our hereditary Fear of Change: 'We know what we've got, but not what we'll get.' Pulling powers are supposed to represent our needs, wishes and dreams as consumers, users and citizens. The pull on the stubborn donkey's rope (Fig. 1.4). Now, if all three parts in this equation cooperate, very swift development can occur (as for instance in the case of email and SMS services).

Powers of inertia (regarded as a necessary evil by progress- and profit-hungry electronics companies) do however, play an important societal function in the sense that they prevent us from throwing ourselves blindly into the arms of new and unproven technologies. They give us time to talk, analyse, assess and (hopefully) make well-founded political decisions in the demo-cratic tradition. Let me now try to analyse digital cinema from this perspective.

To begin with, who's pushing? Definitely not Hollywood (with the exception of George Lucas). D-cinema projector and server manufacturers? HD camera manufacturers? Well, they of course need to recoup their R&D costs as soon as possible and make the profits that keep their shareholders happy. However, they do not hold much political clout. (See further in Patrick von Sychowski's Chapter 8, 'The Digital Future of Cinema'.)

What are the powers of inertia? The fear of change within Hollywood and the international cinema owner's associations represent a tremendous stalling power. The day they decide to officially press the GO button for

Fig 1.4   The PIP (Push – Inertia – Pull) model (illustrated by Lasse Svanberg)

D-cinema (and start pushing) a major part of the 125 000 cinema screens world wide will go digital within ten years. I think.

And the pull powers? Consumer needs? There are none as I see it. I cannot imagine that average cinemagoers are longing to see their favourite films as pixels projected digitally from a server instead of as silver halide crystals imbedded in transparent acetate film. When the transition occurs they will probably not notice the difference (at least not in big-city first release cinemas). Presumably not even with 4K projection in the distant future. That represents a dilemma for cinema owners and distributors. Yesterday's cinemagoers gladly paid a bit more for the tickets when sound film, colour and wide screen films were introduced because it bought them added value in clearly visible and audible forms. Not so with D-cinema. With the exception, of course, of smaller rural cinemas used to a diet of old, scratched and dirty film prints (see the 'Folkets Hus Digital Houses Project' in Chapter 7).

So – not much push and no pull. The D-cinema market of today is in other words dominated by a donkey and the fear of change? (Not in China and India though.)

The Future

Will cinematographic film finally die? Yes, of course. We are at the beginning of a vicious circle where the demand for 35 mm film (both camera and print film) will gradually decrease. Lower demand usually lead to higher prices and 35 mm film will in that case become a more and more elite medium. The length of this phase-out period depends on how soon the digital alternatives can become both cheaper and better than film. And we are not there yet, far from it.

Isn't it time to revaluate the 'film' concept? What shall we call a 'film' that has never passed a film camera, a film lab or a cinema film projector and spends its entire life in the digital domain? This definition problem will become more apparent when these 'films' can be watched digitally in an E- or D-cinema near you.

The Achilles heel of digital recording media is their fragility (not to say worthlessness) as media for long-time archiving. It should be in the interest of today's filmmakers that their HDCAM tapes, hard discs or digital masters will be in a re-useable condition 10–15 years from now, especially if their budget does not allow a safety master on 35 mm film. When we *do* have national networks of D-cinemas the producer's motivation to invest in a film safety master will be even lower. This important problem is thoroughly and intelligently dealt with in the last chapter of this book, 'Archiving Digital Media' by Paul Read.

Why is digital technology trying so hard to copy the film tradition? The first non-linear editing computers tried to resemble Steenbeck film-editing tables.

The first D-cinema projectors looked like traditional film projectors with a gigantic Xenon lamp-house hooked onto them (now being smaller self-contained units). Why should E- and D-cinemas use projectors at all (an old-fashioned and expensive solution, especially considering that the lamp unit costs 6000 Euro and has to be changed after some 400 screenings)? Why is the old 'film look' so desirable when you shoot digitally?

I think that these attitudes will pass away in the near future and digital film production, distribution and exhibition will free itself of the burden of old, stale film traditions and establish identities, looks, networks, distribution channels and storytelling techniques of their own. Will the road to this new creative freedom be lined with the ruins of old film bastions and left-overs from the Hollywood hegemony?

A Note About This Book

This book does not reflect or promote any official standpoints of the European Digital Cinema Forum (EDCF). The opinions voiced here are the opinions of the individual authors (including me of course). In my work as Editor I have tried to create a varied palette of opinions and experiences. You will see the same type of problems approached from different angles and filtered through different personal temperaments. I hope it will give you a better view of the 'agony and ecstasy' of digital film production, at a stage when film production is about to go through its most radical period of change since sound film was introduced in the late 1920s. The Third Wave.

The book has a specific focus – professional HD-based film production for the big cinema screen. Film production is the concern of the DoP – the Director of Photography. Had the term been spelled out everywhere, the book would have been a page or two longer, so the abbreviation is used. It can also be shortened to DP and, to add to the confusion, it may very well become DoI or DI (Director of Imaging) in the near future, since that better covers what today's DoPs actually do during their working hours.

Now, before I hand over to the other contributors to this book, I would like to end this Introduction with my favourite story in the techno-sceptical spirit – and with particular address to photo-chemical fundamentalists, digi-freaks and neophiles who think that they have ready-made answers to how today's Digital Dilemma should be solved.

Albert Einstein was for a time professor in physics at the University of Vienna. It was time for the students' annual written tests and his secretary comes rushing into his office and exclaims: 'But dear Professor, these questions are identical to the ones you gave your students the last time. They already know the answers!'

'Doesn't matter', said Einstein calmly. 'I have changed the answers.'

2

The Toolbox

2.1 HD Systems and Cameras, *By Roland Sterner*

Systems

All video systems with a linearity higher than the standard definition (SD) systems NTSC (525 nominal lines, 485 active lines), PAL and SECAM (625 nominal, 576 active) are named high definition, or HD for short. Sony began development of an HD video system in the early 1970s. It had a linearity of 1125 lines and a frame rate of 30 fps. The image was widened to 16:9 to simulate recent wide screen feature films and their compositions and pictorial language. Transmissions were made using this system from the early 1980s. It was a problem making HDVS a world standard, however, since it was a completely analogue system, and it had to be designed in two electronic specifications – for 60 Hz AC and for 50 Hz AC. The system was demonstrated and evaluated all over the world, but the television markets were reluctant to concentrate on it, since the consumer receivers were both very expensive and bulky. Flat-panel HD screens were at this time a futuristic dream. Furthermore, the system required the replacement of all existing electronic equipment, circuits, mixers and even cables.

Not until the arrival of high power electronic circuits and digital signal processing did the HD technology develop significantly.

The different HD formats are usually described with the number of vertical lines followed by a letter, either i or p. These letters indicate if the scanning of the lines is done interlaced (i.e. every other line in two fields which together make a video image) or progressive, where all lines are scanned in succession. In many contexts, the frame rate is also given, for example 1080/25p or 720/60p.

The system that has been used for most feature film applications, Sony CineAlta, is a 1080p system, which means that the image has a height of 1080 lines and every line has a horizontal resolution of 1920 pixels. For HDTV broadcast use, some HD cameras can be set to a lower resolution, 720×1280 pixels. For HD cinema applications, the frame rate of the camera is set to the actual production standard in the country of production. In NTSC countries, 24 fps is used, while PAL countries prefer 25 fps for problem-free editing.

13

Most cameras in use prior to the time of writing have had their video signals recorded on to tape. To make it possible for the tape to store the enormous amount of data required for HD images, the signal must be compressed. This gives a deterioration of the image, compared to what the camera itself can produce. Recent developments permit the data from the camera to be recorded uncompressed, or with a much lower compression than before. This requires the use of large hard discs, stand-alone recorders (some of which require compression) or RAM memories, perhaps with a limited time for recording, but not much less than a film magazine of 400 or 1000 ft.

Requirements

Most of the cameras now in use for HD cinema are constructed for HDTV broadcast use. The requirements for a HD camera intended for feature film photography are very definite and demanding, since every experienced cinematographer expects the camera to behave in similar ways to a film camera, 35 mm or Super 16 mm, if a change in shooting technology could be considered.

The following properties for a HD camera are necessary to give the cinematographer all the freedom and opportunities to work in a cinematic way:

- Capacity to produce film-like images, the elusive 'film look'.
- Excellent image sharpness and resolution high enough for good detail reproduction even in long shots, combined with an excellent reproduction of colour.
- Possibility of achieving a shallow depth of field.
- Colour viewfinder to have absolute control over the recorded image.
- Variable frame rate in small increments.
- Wide enough exposure latitude for high contrast subjects.
- A wide variety of high quality lenses of different focal lengths, including zooms.
- Low camera noise, to avoid the use of a soft blimp on the camera.
- Film camera accessories such as matte boxes, follow focus, viewfinder extensions etc.
- Possibility to change colours and exposure in post-production, like film grading.

The 'Film Look'

There are several basic areas where the differences between film and HD cameras are quite obvious. There is always that old question on how to achieve the 'film look' from a video system. This look is hard to define, but an early crude attempt was to give the video image, consisting of 50 or 60 fields per second, an artificial 'strobed' look to imitate the 24 frames per second of 35 mm film in cinema projection. Modern HD cameras can be set to different frame rates, and the dividing of the frame in fields disappears when the camera is set to 24 or 25 fps progressive scanning. This gives the well-known film-like and slightly strobing effect in object and camera movements.

All video cameras nowadays have an image sensor made from a great number of small light sensitive dots, pixels, but the number of these dots cannot be compared to the number of grains in a film emulsion. Furthermore, the CCD pixels stay in the same place all the time, while the film grains are changing places for every frame of film. Exactly what this means for the film look is perhaps hard to evaluate, but something relevant for the 'film look' could emanate from this fact.

Image Sharpness, Resolution and Colour Quality

The three standard 2/3 inch CCD image sensors get their images through a beam-splitting prism which divides the light from the subject into its RGB components. Although this is an old and well-tried technique, it would be better if the image from the lens could hit the sensor directly. This means that a new type of sensor must be constructed, to be able to record all three colours simultaneously. Through many years of research and development in stills photography and satellite imaging, this is about to happen very soon.

An ordinary HD camera has a resolution of 1080×1920 pixels and records the video signal with a colour depth of 8 bits. This is perhaps sufficient for HDTV broadcasts but not when the images are transferred to 35 mm film in Arri Laser Recorders and other machines for theatrical release. Many graders in the labs, who are trying to make release prints from the 35 mm negatives, have complained about the limited possibilities to fine-tune the colours, especially skin tones. One step on their printer grading scale makes the skin tones change significantly. If the colour depth is increased, the data flow will be insurmountably large. However, through the very fast developments in data storage techniques, this problem can be solved in a very short time.

Another source of image deterioration is the compression of the video signal in order to record it in a practical way on the built-in recorder. The most recent HD cameras have a new approach to this problem. The signal from the camera consists of raw data from the charge coupled device (CCD) sensors, data that can be processed later to form the required image. In this way, a range of about nine stops can be achieved (see Panasonic below).

Some recent cameras (Viper FilmStream, DALSA, Arri D-20) do not have a built-in tape recorder, but require the signals to be recorded on separate hard discs or other recording devices. Considering the rapidly increasing storage capabilities of hard discs, it is wise not to limit the recording capabilities to a VTR built in the camera. A new HD recorder from Sony, the HDCAM-SR, records the video signal in 4:4:4 mode without sub-sampling or pre-filtering.

There is also a recording device called CineRAM for HD cameras where uncompressed signals can be recorded. Made by Baytech in California, it recognizes all recent HD formats. It is mounted on the back of the camera like an on-board battery. This means that no cables have to be connected to the camera while shooting Steadicam and other types of mobile scenes, or when shooting hand-held in crowd scenes where the cables would be in the way. The CineRAM can record 2.7 minutes of uncompressed output from Viper or F-950 Dual Link. This means that the memory must be emptied at regular intervals, like the changing of film magazines. When Single Link output from Panasonic Varicam is recorded, the capacity extends to 10 minutes. Data can be downloaded via Dual Gigabit IP/Ethernet for immediate evaluation or previewing.

Depth of Field

Next, and quite difficult to achieve, is emulating the limited depth of field of 35 mm film cameras, which is a most important part of the visual interpretation in fiction films. Every movie uses a limited depth of field to concentrate the images and control the spectator's reading of the image content.

Since most video cameras have an image sensor of 2/3 inch size, the frame is actually smaller than Super 16 (10×6 mm for video, compared to 12.7×7.5 mm for Super 16 and 21×11.3 for 35 mm film 1:1.85). This means that the focal lengths of the HD lenses are considerably shorter than those intended for Super 16 use, and hence the larger depth of field. The obvious solution to this problem would be to increase the image area of the HD camera, and the most recent developments in HD camera design have done just that. Some types of camera have an image sensor the same size as a 35 mm image, which allows for the use of regular 35 mm lenses, and since this type of sensor can record all three colours, there is no need for a beam-splitting prism.

Another method is to use a device constructed and marketed by P+S Technik in Munich. This device is called Pro35 Digital and accepts 35 mm PL mount lenses or Nikon mount lenses. The image from these lenses is captured on a rotating ground glass and re-photographed with a relaying macro lens adapted to give an image with the correct size for the sensors of the HD camera. This means that the depth of field is exactly the same as it would have been on a 35 mm film frame. The macro lens has its own iris for setting the exposure, which means that the front lens can be set wide open or very slightly stepped down, for the desired depth of field (see further in the next part of this chapter, HD Camera Testing).

The Viewfinder

Most HD cameras are plagued with a primitive black-and-white viewfinder, like ordinary video cameras have had for a long time. The reason why most video cameras have a black-and-white monitor viewfinder is that it shows the image sharpness more accurately than colour monitors of this minute size. This means that a large size colour monitor must be present on the set for critical judgement of the image. This is easy in a studio, but very complicated in daylight exteriors, where huge black shields (or a small tent) must be used to block off the daylight from the screen. The latest Sony model (HDC F-950), however, has a colour viewfinder with a zoom function for critical focusing.

Very recent developments in HD camera design (see below under Arri and DALSA) have permitted the removal of the beam-splitting prism and thus making it possible to use a rotating mirror viewfinder exactly like in a film camera. The image is captured on a ground glass and can be evaluated in a way that all cinematographers are familiar with. For the last 50 years nearly all film cameras have been equipped with a reflex viewfinder system, which allows the operator to see the image in colour and to check focus during shooting. The disadvantage is that most mirror reflex systems deflect the image to the ground glass behind the lens, which means that the image can be very dark when the lens is stopped down or ND filters are used.

Variable Frame Rate

An old problem with video technology is the difficulty in changing the frame rate of the camera. The established visual language of film often contains scenes in slow or fast motion. Virtually all film cameras, even very simple models, can easily change frame rate, while all standard PAL video cameras only record in 25 fps (50 fields per second), and NTSC in 30 fps (60 or more precisely 59.94 fields). The old way of making slow motion from video was to double the existing frames, which increased the blur around fast-moving objects. The development of digital signal processing has permitted the most recent camera models to record in different frame rates. The Panasonic HD DVCPRO camera Varicam has got its name from this feature, but there are other cameras with the same option.

With the Varicam the frame rate can be varied from 4 to 60 fps and the 'shutter speed' from 3 to 350 degrees, for various conscious strobing effects. However, the recording on the tape is always carried out at 60 fps, and conversion to different production standards is done in an external frame rate converter.

The Viper FilmStream HD camera can produce various slow motion effects by shooting in the 720/60 mode and having the image signals processed in post-production.

Exposure Latitude

An experienced cinematographer uses the full latitude of exposure when shooting film. The range of a modern 35 mm negative can embrace 11–12 stops, while video cameras have a limited range of about eight stops. This may require more work controlling the lighting of the scene, for instance the use of ND filters in windows and in front of practicals, and strong fill light in daylight exteriors.

Some recent cameras, however, do not process the video image in the camera, but export raw data from the image sensors. In this way the gamma correction can be adjusted later. This method requires a separate signal recording facility, such as an array of hard discs.

Lenses

The first HD cameras were equipped with high quality video zoom lenses made for HDTV applications, but they were not satisfactory when the images were transferred to 35 mm film or projected digitally on a large screen. The next step was to use lenses made for 35 mm cinematography and reduce their image size with a special optical converter to fit the CCD image area of 6 × 10 mm in the HD camera. This gave the lenses more speed but the optical reduction system did not improve their sharpness.

Panavision realized this, and designed lenses with a resolution high enough for cinema applications. Now there are several series of prime lenses on the market for HD cameras, from Fujinon, Canon and Zeiss, as well as zooms of different ranges from well-known manufacturers. Panavision Primo Digital® lenses are designed to give 2.5 times better performance than their cine counterparts. They can safely be used at maximum aperture (T 1.6–1.9) in order to reduce depth of field. The zooms are made with the overlapping ranges 6–27 mm and 25–112 mm. There is also an 11× zoom 9.5–105 mm. The prime lenses have focal lengths of 5, 7, 10, 14, 20 and 35 mm. For comparison: a lens for 2/3 inch HD with a focal length of 5 mm corresponds to a 12.5 mm lens for 35 mm Academy and a 6, 6 mm lens for Super 16. A 14 mm HD lens can be compared to a 35 mm lens for Academy and 18.5 mm for Super 16.

In April 2002 Zeiss introduced their DigiPrimes, with the focal lengths 5, 7, 10, 14, 20 and 40 mm, supplemented in 2003 with 28 and 70 mm. The lens speeds are all around T1.6–T1.9, and they are designed to give excellent sharpness wide open.

Zoom lenses of a quality optimized for HD cinema are made by the highly reputed lens makers Cooke and Angénieux. The Cooke zoom is a modification of their renowned 18–100 mm for 35 mm, but in HD version its range is 8–46 mm. Maximum aperture is T1.7. The lens has a newly designed mechanism for extreme critical adjustment of the back-focus.

The Angénieux 12× zoom Optimo has also an HD version 9.7–16 mm T1.6. It is reported that it has no zoom effect when focus is changed, in spite of its long range.

Fuji in Japan has two new zoom lenses, reportedly commissioned for the new *Star Wars: Episode III* movie. Several scenes in the previous film were shot with Fujinon zooms, and the result was so good that the new film will be shot entirely with Fujinon lenses. Since the greatest difficulty in zoom design lies in the combination of short focal length, high quality and acceptable size and weight, two lenses were designed. One is a short 3× zoom, 5–15 mm with T1.6, and the other is a 10× zoom 100 mm T1.8. A third Fujinon model in the Super Cine Style Zoom range is the 6–30 mm T1.8. The Fujinon Cine Style prime lenses are available in eight focal lengths from 5 to 54 mm and have a speed of T1.6, except for the wide angle 5 mm, which has a maximum aperture of T2.0.

The HD lens range from Canon comprises two zooms, 7.5–158 mm and 4.7–52 mm, both with maximum aperture of T2.1. Their primes have focal lengths of 5, 9, 14, 24 and 35 mm, with a speed of T1.5 (except for the 5 mm which has T1.7).

Camera Noise

A piece of equipment containing electronic circuits as advanced as an HD camera needs to be effectively cooled with a fan. The noise emanating from the fan (and the video drum in cameras with a built-in VTR) has caused a lot of trouble for sound technicians in cramped shooting environments. The common habit of covering the camera with a soft blimp makes the camera even hotter, and the elongation of the metal parts caused by the heat can affect the critical back focus adjustment. A soft blimp will also cover the sides of the camera where several important switches and monitoring devices are located. The camera makers must find a way to make the cooling more effective without causing disturbing noise. One solution is to make the camera housing larger, to allow more air to flow around the electronic circuits, but that will certainly not be accepted by the users (see further on this aspect in Chapter 3, 'Ingmar Bergman Meets Hi-Tech').

Accessories

The need for the HD cameras to accept film camera accessories was recognized very early. Sony and Panavision formed a cooperation, where Panavision bought 100 Sony HDW-F900 cameras and 'Panavized' them. Six of these modified cameras were used in year 2000 when George Lucas shot *Star Wars: Episode II, The Attack of the Clones* in HD. The modified camera of course accepts all relevant Panavision accessories, like matte boxes, follow focus attachments, viewfinder extension etc. The viewfinder itself is replaced with an enhanced system called Ultraview®.

The large American rental company Clairmont has also made a modification of the Sony HDW-F900, where great effort has been made to stabilize the optical system by exchanging the support for the beam splitter and CCD sensors with stainless steel material, thus minimizing the risk that temperature changes may affect the back focal distance.

A very radical view of HD camera construction has been taken by Arri in Munich. They have designed a special HD sensor pack for a standard 35 mm film camera (Arri 435) to be placed where the film magazine normally is! The image is captured on a single large format CMOS sensor, allowing the use of standard 35 mm lenses. All well-known features are kept on the camera, including the capability to use all standard accessories.

Post-production

There is a tendency in recent camera models to record as much image data as possible, without compression or any other processing in the camera, either by recording on separate units like hard discs, or having the built-in VTR record raw data to be processed later. This is similar to the working practice in film production to give the negative a full exposure, and decide later in post-production how the images will look in the release print or telecine. The rapid developments in data recording capacity will make this method of working more common in the future.

Recent Camera Models

Sony

Sony, due to their many years of experience in the HD field, was in the market early with its HD camera HDW-F900 for the 24p system, later renamed CineAlta. The first HD recorded feature film to reach cinemas was shot with this camera. It was the Swedish *Hem ljuva Hem* (Home Sweet Home) in 2000. The system records the images with the resolution of

1080 × 1920, and it can be set to eight frame rates: 23.98p, 24p, 25p, 29.97p, 30p, 50i, 59.94i and 60i.

A somewhat simpler model called HDW-F750 has just two settings for image recording – 25p and 50i – and is primarily intended for HDTV applications in PAL countries. The top of the CineAlta line model, HDC-F950, gives uncompressed 1080×1920 HD 4:4:4 in its RGB component outlet. To obtain highest possible quality, the signal must be recorded on to hard discs or stand-alone recorders. One model is intended for field use, the other for studio use, both with the MPEG-4 compression algorithm. The George Lucas production *Star Wars: Episode III* is shot with this camera, which also has a high definition colour viewfinder with a zoom function. In progressive mode, the camera can record in frame rates of 1–24 fps.

Panasonic HD

Panasonic has an HD variation of its DVCPRO system, 720×1280. The camera AJ-HDC27FE has some unique features, including variable frame rates and external gamma correction.

Fig 2.1   The Sony HDW-F900, film-styled

The frame rate can be set from 4 to 60 fps in single increments. An external frame rate converter can process and line-convert the recorded signal to the desired production standard, from 720p to 1080p, 24, 25 or 60 fps, or down-convert to SD video 576/50i.

When the camera is set to a recording mode called F.REC the VTR records raw data from the image sensors. The gamma can then be varied by external processing in an HD Gamma Corrector for different effects, including adapting the image quality for transfer to film. Through this process the exposure range can be extended to nine steps. For the operator's convenience, the camera accepts several accessories, such as matte boxes and follow focus from Arri and Chrosziel.

Viper

Thomson has realized that a weak point in the chain is the recording of HD video signals on to tape, and their cameras, both the HDTV broadcast camera LDK6000 Mk II and the cinema model Viper FilmStream, are not equipped with tape recorders. The signals from the camera can be fed to any recording system depending on the intended use of the material. For studio applications, the signals can be recorded directly on to hard discs, without any signal compression.

The CCD sensors, each containing 9.2 million pixels, are working in frame transfer mode, which requires a mechanical shutter. Through a combination of sub-pixels, a 1:2.35 image can be recorded without the use of anamorphic optics. The signals from the three CCDs are led to 12 bit analogue-to-digital converters, and are through logarithmic calculations converted to 10 bit RGB data. This means that each colour is defined in 1024 steps, instead of the 256 steps obtained with 8 bit processing. Since the complete information from the image sensors is recorded, a very high data flow must be handled: 2978 gigabytes per second, sent through double HD-SDI cables. If 30 minutes of material is shot in one day (corresponding to three 1000 ft rolls of 35 mm film), 5360 gigabytes of data must be recorded! There are already hard discs on the market that can record several terabytes of data, and if even larger amounts of data must be stored, there is always the possibility to make tape back-ups. For HDTV broadcast applications, the Viper also has YUV option over a single HD-SDI cable, and with this option normal signal processing can be carried out in the camera.

Dalsa

The Canadian company DALSA, from Waterloo, Ontario, has shown a pro-totype of a camera named Origin, which promises to be something extra.

The company specializes in large image sensors for stills photography, satellites etc. and they have made an image sensor with four times higher resolution than HD: 4046×2048 or 8.2 million pixels compared to 2.07 million for HD. The size of the sensor is larger than a 35 mm frame, and it can be masked down to required image proportions: 1:1.85 or 1:2.35. The data flow is very high, and requires separate processing to obtain maximum quality. Aside from the regular 4:4:4 signal the camera can also produce a 'proxy' signal, which gives a lower resolution image intended for offline editing.

Arri

After several years of experimentation and evaluating many comparisons between film and HD technology, Arri has shown a prototype of a new camera called D-20. It looks like an Arri 435 film camera with the magazine substituted for an HD image capturing device. All well-known features of a film camera are retained–the lenses, the matte box and follow focus and the reflex viewfinder. The single image sensor, a CMOS with 6.2 million pixels, has the size of a 35 mm film frame. The separation to the primary colours is done by a Bayer Mask, which gives each third pixel an RGB colour. After the necessary interpolation, the horizontal resolution is 1920 pixels.

The camera has a high speed capability which results in very high bit rates. The data flow from the image sensor is not internally processed or

Fig 2.2   The Canadian Dalsa camera with 8.2 megapixel sensor

Fig 2.3   A second prototype of Arri's D-20 camera.

compressed. However, it must be externally processed before it can form an image, which is somewhat similar to film processing!

JVC

The smallest HD camera on the market comes from JVC in Japan. It is called JY-HD10 and has a single 1/3 inch image sensor with 1.18 mega pixels. It can record both progressively and interlaced. The resolution is 960 × 659 pixels, which is considerably smaller than the standard HD 720 × 1280. The recording is done on Mini-DV cassettes. The camera is also capable of recording in standard definition DV 4:3 and 16:9.

Conclusion

Most of the disadvantages that affected the quality of HD compared to film are about to disappear by the most recent developments in HD camera design. The use of large format CCD and CMOS image sensors, with a frame size of 35 mm film, allow for the use of well-known reliable lenses and gives an acceptable depth of field that it is possible to control. The cinematographers can also see their images in a mirror reflex viewfinder, as they are used to. This stage of development can be compared with the transition in the early 1950s from three-strip Technicolor with its beam-splitter camera, to the multi-layered colour films. On Panavision's new Genesis camera, see Michael Brennan's question, number 36, page 38.

New types of hard discs, blue laser recorders or RAM memories with high capacity may allow recording of a high data flow which eliminates the necessity to compress the signals.

Presumably the colour depth will be higher, which gives a more natural colour palette and makes life easier for the film graders when they make the release prints.

Full flexibility in the choice of frame rate, for special effects or creating subtle mood impressions, will become available.

One factor that is difficult to predict is the cost of HD cameras. It is possible that their price will fall off rapidly, owing to the very fast technical developments, and yet because of these ongoing developments, the cameras will be made in limited quantities, which will account for a high price per item. But if a new and better HD cinema system comes on the market, the 'old' cameras can always be used for HDTV broadcasts.

2.2   HD Camera Testing, *By Hans Hansson*

Before shooting starts it is important to thoroughly test the camera(s), lenses and other camera-related equipment to be used on the production, in order to avoid technical 'surprises' and to get familiar with the image quality. Devote at least a full working day to this; make the technical tests described below and shoot a few scenes on locations and in lighting conditions similar to scenes that appear in the script. Then evaluate this material together with the director and the person who will be responsible for 'digital post'.

Choice of Lenses

Some DoPs prefer prime lenses, others prefer zoom lenses. There is today also a third alternative; P+S Techniks Pro 35 Digital, a lens adapter which makes it possible to use 35 mm film lenses on 2/3 inch video cameras and maintain the field of view and limited depth of field of the film camera lenses.

Adjusting Back-focus with a Siemens Star

Make sure that the camera is 'zeroed', in other words set at the manufacturer's basic setting for functions and menus, or the menu recommended by the camera rental facility. Start by testing the lenses and adjusting back-focus. Turn the camera on and let it get warm, which takes about 10 minutes. White- and black-balance the camera.

Fig 2.4 P+S Techniks Pro 35 Digital adapter for 35 mm film lenses on ²/₃ inch video cameras.

Place a Siemens star at 2–3 m distance and light it so that correct exposure is achieved at full stop. You can also use the setting Gain –3 dB to reduce sensitivity. In order to get best possible image of the Siemens star you should use a large monitor and turn off colour (Chrominance).

When using zoom lenses you should start by zooming in all the way and then set focus with front focus (the focusing scale on the lens). Then zoom out to the shortest focal length and set the focus with the back-focus adjustment. Then zoom in again and set the focus with the focusing scale on the lens. Zoom out again and adjust the focus with back-focus. Repeat this process until full resolution is achieved within the entire range of the zoom lens. Then lock the back-focus ring carefully. Check that the focusing scale on the lens is accurate by measuring the distance to the Siemens star with a tape measure; 2 m should be a suitable working distance. Please note that for 'film styled' zoom lenses the distance is measured from the focal plane, for so-called ENG (Electronic News Gathering) zoom lenses it is measured from the front lens.

For shorter fixed focal lenses (prime lenses) the Siemens star should be placed 1 m from the focal plane and the distance scale set on 1 m. Then adjust back-focus for best resolution. For longer focal lengths the distance between the camera and the star should be increased to 2–3 m. (Test charts with Siemens star can be ordered through www.esser-test-charts.com/video/index.htm.)

Adjusting Back-focus with a Collimator

The collimator is an optical instrument which makes the adjustment of back-focus both easier and more accurate. For HD lenses they are manufactured by Carl Zeiss and Century Optics. The collimator has a back-lit Siemens star which is projected via a lens system through the camera lens. Front focus should be set on infinity and iris at full stop (or stopped down one stop). The light level in the collimator is then adjusted until correct exposure is achieved. Then back-focus is set for maximum resolution. For zoom lenses focus should be checked for both the longest and the shortest focal lengths.

Adjusting back-focus with a collimator gives maximal precision and is in many ways superior to the test-chart method described above, especially if you are on the set and in the middle of shooting.

P+S Pro Digital Images Converter

To adjust for best focus mount a film lens on the Images converter. Place a focusing chart at a reasonable distance and set the film lens focusing scale

Fig 2.5   Carl Zeiss Sharp Max collimator

at, for example, 2 metres. Turn the converter ON. Open the adjustable ND filter to position 0, turn the iris down to around T4 and adjust the light to correct exposure. Unscrew the lever on the back-focus ring and turn the ring to adjust for best sharpness. Tighten the lever at the back-focus ring.

In the field, if a reliable test chart is not available, adjust the back-focus the following way. Use a white chart at a reasonable distance to fill the image. Turn the converter OFF and open the ND filter to position 0. Close the iris of the film lens far enough to allow the video camera to show the grain pattern of the ground glass. Unscrew the lever on the back-focus ring and turn the ring to adjust sharpness. When the grain pattern is sharp, the image converter is accurately adjusted to the camera.

Lens Sharpness Tests

In order to evaluate the resolution power of a specific lens a special test chart with linear or circular patterns should be filmed. The chart should be filmed at a specified distance depending on the focal length of the lens. The Putora Sharpness Indicator Test Charts (Fig. 2.6) are easy to use, but there are several other brands. If the end result of the production will be 35 mm release prints you have to make a print from the negative and project it on a cinema screen in order to make a good judgement of the sharpness of the lenses. It is also recommended to shoot a few scenes in realistic lighting in settings described in the script. This way you will see how the lenses react in strong back-light and how sensitive they are to flare.

Exposure

Correct exposure is of *vital* importance on HD productions. Overexposed images give burned-out highlights which cannot be dealt with in post-production. As a guidance for correct exposure the viewfinder has two so-called Zebra patterns. These patterns indicate a certain level of the video signal and can be pre-set in the menu. You can use one of them or both. When using both, the first Zebra pattern can, for instance, indicate a video level of 95% (white with detail) and the other, 67–70% (Caucasian skin tone).

If a waveform monitor is available you will get more exact measurements of the video signal plus a graphic depiction of the camera picture which gives you better exposure control. Today there are compact LCD monitors for HD which can both show the camera image and function as a waveform monitor. With the monitor connected to the camera, the camera operator has constant control of both camera image and video signal.

Exposure assessment during camera tests should be done with test charts with double grey scales, so-called ship charts. The grey scale test chart is

Fig 2.6 Putora Sharpness Chart

used in conjunction with a waveform monitor to adjust the light response characteristics (video levels of gamma) of the camera and to ensure that these characteristics are matched in all three colour channels. It is also used to adjust shading and flare compensation.

The 11-step Grey Scale Chart is an extended range test chart intended for use with high-performance video cameras. The chart consists of two arrays of 11 neutral grey patches or 'chips' ranging in reflectance from 2% to approximately 90% (approximately 5.5 f-stops). The arrays are arranged so that one increases in reflectance from right to left and the other from left to right. The strips are mounted on a uniform grey background with a reflectance of 16%. A black-white-black test object in the centre of the chart provides a black (0.5% reflectance) reference for adjusting dead black level in amplifier set-up as well as a 'super-white' (90% reflectance) patch for setting peak video in many applications.

The black regions can also be used for flare compensation adjustment. If ENG lenses are used, check that the automatic exposure control gives correct exposure. Adjustments of the automatic exposure control can be done in the menus.

2.3 The 45 Most Frequent Questions and Statements on HD Production, *By Michael Brennan*

1   What is HD?

'High definition' (HD) is a very general term used to describe cameras, editing equipment, lenses, transmission and recording formats. The one common element is that HD offers the promise of higher quality than standard definition. There are many HD recording and transmission formats with different resolutions and frame rates. There are no standards for HD lenses, or standards for compression. For instance, a low resolution standard definition image can be upconverted to an HD signal and then forever more be correctly termed a HD picture. So sometimes HD is less than it should be.

Film can be transferred to HD for editing. A so called 'HD production' could be shot on film and promoted as a HD or digital production. The term HD is also being loosely used to describe the upcoming range of 2k and 4k digital motion picture cameras.

2   Do You Need Less Light When You Shoot HD?

In controlled situations you will use the same number of lights as with film. In uncontrolled, low light situations it is possible to utilize available light more effectively than on 35 mm film. This is because there is much greater depth of field with HD format than 35 mm film. This is solely to do with the small size of the HD sensor, not any shortcoming in the sensitivity of film. For modest production budgets on HD an acceptable depth of field can be utilized using ambient street light with the addition of a few key and back lights on the subject. But if shooting outdoors the amount of light needed to balance sunlight is the same, if not more on HD as film. So although it is possible to pick up a HD camera, switch it on and record a picture, without careful lighting the result can be nothing more than HD home movies.

3   Do You Need Less Crew with HD?

If you need an image for a large screen presentation that is steady and sharp you must use a 35 mm style crew (retrained to use a digital camera). The same goes for TV drama work. It is possible to work with less crew but you will be limited in your range of shots. For instance an operator with an assistant and director can shoot general views, but pulling focus by relying on the viewfinder is difficult.

4   "HD Tapes Can be Damaged by X-rays or Metal Detectors"

HD tapes are perfectly safe being transported through airport security scanners and X-ray machines. The HD recording is more difficult to erase than Digibeta or Beta SP. A metal detector is thousands of times less powerful than what is required to damage a HD tape. Even a hand-held metal detector, passing directly over a tape, will not damage it.

5   "HD CCDs Are Damaged by Airline Travel"

Anecdotal evidence suggests that gamma rays will damage pixels in camcorders. It seems that if a camera is going to have a problem, it has it on its first or second flight. If it survives its first few flights the CCD seems not to be affected by subsequent flights. This has been the case with standard definition cameras in the past few years where less than 1% of cameras have been found on delivery (or shortly after) to have 'dead' pixels. However an early model HD camera in the space shuttle has lost many pixels perhaps due to its prolonged exposure to gamma rays. One must be vigilant if the camera is new.

6   How Good is the Audio Recording on an HD Camcorder?

Better than DAT. Four channels can be available with an adapter on a camcorder.

7   Do I Use a Clapper with HD?

If the cast and crew are feeling 'clapper withdrawal symptoms' then yes, even if you are recording sound on camera. However the continuity person should make a note of timecode regardless of whether the clapper is used or not. The director and editor are far more likely to refer to timecode than clapper. A producer should consider that introducing HD, like any new technology challenging an established profession, is more to do with people and jobs than pixels and compression.

8   What is Negative Fill?

Negative fill is achieved by blocking out ambient light from the subject. As CCDs respond well in the shadows it is not uncommon on location to use negative fill to darken one side of the subject to create modelling.

9   Is There a Difference in Lighting for HD Rather than Film or SD?

HD 'sees' more detail than standard definition (SD) especially in the shadows. It is possible to exploit this with subtle lighting. On the other hand, highlights burn out more readily than film so the DoP must be careful to control highlights, through makeup, filtration, post-production techniques and careful control of lighting. Some lighting effects do not work at all in HD. High key is particularly difficult. A combination of lighting and post effects should be explored to create your look.

10   Do I Need a Big HD Monitor to Make Good HD Pictures?

An inexperienced DoP or operator will need a good monitor. Makeup, props director and gaffer love the big monitor in a studio as it allows them to do their job more efficiently and effectively, especially on limited budgets. If the 24 inch monitor is impractical a 14 inch CRT monitor will give a reliable idea of focus, gamma, highlight and shadow detail. A 9 inch monitor is a good representation of colour and gamma. However it is pointless using the monitor for critical evaluation unless the DoP is under a black cloth or the monitor is in a dark room. And don't forget to remove your sunglasses.

A range of HD LCD and TFT displays are being released that offer good resolution and will be suitable for checking focus and examining detail. They are unlikely to be suitable to aid fine control of lighting or adjusting the colorimetry or gamma of the camera. However, as they are less bulky and cost less than heavy HD CRT monitors they will become popular. Using a large flat screen and a mid-size say, 14 inch CRT is a good compromise for location work.

11   Do HD Cameras have a Problem with Red?

Panavision cameras have a different IR (infrared filter) than is installed at the factory by Sony. This means more infrared light hits the CCDs. This has led to some confusion that there is a problem with non-Panavized cameras.

12   Why Shoot HD if there is No HD Transmission?

For the same reason we prefer to use 35 mm film rather than 16 mm for TV. The improved quality of the 35 mm format can be seen even on an SD transmission. The same applies to HD. There is greater degree of manipulation in post-production, i.e. reframing. The benefits of a high resolution, low noise image are also apparent when encoding to DVD. If operated in progressive mode HD cameras capture motion in a way that is similar to the film look. HD transmission is available in USA, Japan, Australia and in a limited fashion in Europe. HD quality distribution to large screen or HD flat screen is becoming increasingly common across a wide range of industries beyond broadcasting.

13   Can HD Record in Slow Motion?

The limit for a camcorder at the moment is Varicam 60 fps at 1220×720. A 1920×1080 60i recording can be deinterlaced and turned into a 60p recording at the cost of lowering the resolution. Ikegami have demonstrated a true 120fps 720p camera that uses a hard disc to record the images. A 1920×1080 camera running at 60p is available from Thomson. There is a range of digital super slo mo cameras using single chip imagers of up to 2k resolution, that are capable of up to 3000 frames per second. The images, usually totalling two or three thousand frames are stored in RAM, then downloaded.

14   "Video Lenses are Inferior to Film Lenses"

Second generation HD lenses and primes are superior to 35 mm lenses in just about every way. As the size of the image plane is much smaller than 35 mm all the resolving power has to be fine-tuned into a small image plane, so both mechanically and optically they are technically superior to 35 mm lenses. Second and third generation HD lenses are now available that virtually eliminate breathing and are adequate for TV and feature work. More expensive zooms and primes should be considered if budget permits.

15   "Panavision Lenses are Best"

No one to date has done the side by side test, but Fuji's new Super zooms T1.6 are as fast as the big Panavision lenses. In respect of prime lenses, Zeiss and Fuji have superb glass and Canon have a new set of primes. Panavision have adapted their lenses to B4 mount.

16   Should I Record Sound on Camera?

Definitely. You will be able to start your digitizing immediately. On tight budgets a post-production supervisor can schedule the offline or online independently of any sound work. On tight budgets it is possible to do a rough cut with sync and including basic track laying in the offline. Once the pictures are locked all audio channels can be lifted from the online for the sound dub. Expect more audio track laying to take place in the offline as onlines are becoming more audio feature rich.

17   What about the Adapters that Convert 35 mm Lenses to HD?

There are two options. The Angenieux adapter is 200 mm in length and is T1.6 and inverts the image, which can be corrected with appropriate additional hardware of a f900 or at the flick of a switch on the Varicam. The other options utilize a fast spinning ground glass where the image from the 35 mm lens is focused. The image from the ground glass is re-photographed to fit the smaller HD sensor. The result is a soft look with texture. These systems typically reduce effective aperture by one and a half stops.

18   Does HD Strobe more than Film?

No. It captures motion in a very similar way. Some people get disturbed watching the monitor when the camera is being set up and often panned around very quickly. This is not something you see watching film dailies of course. Also if watching a pan on a monitor from a distance the edges of frame can take your attention rather than the subject. Next time you are at the cinema watch the edges of frame not the subject during a pan and you will see strobing. A camera operator who is new to video will need time to acclimatize to an HD viewfinder.

19 "Film Guys can't Handle HD!"

Some old dogs will learn new tricks, others will not. An alternative to expecting a DoP who has never shot video simply to adapt and cope is to have a video operator or a DoP who has worked on HD as part of the crew. At the moment there are not enough experienced HD hands–so get whoever you can to help.

20 Can Video Guys Shoot HD?

A 'video guy' will know how the camera works and have a sensitivity toward CCDs' limited contrast range. He will be able to troubleshoot any problems and not make silly mistakes. However, he may not have experience in framing for a big screen or working with a focus puller. In the United States there has been very little drama shot on video whereas in other parts of the world electronic cinematography has existed using Digibeta for many years. An 'Electronic Cinematography' set up is similar to film, with film style lenses focus pullers etc.

21 Should I Shoot Straight and Achieve the Look I Want in Post?

If you don't know video very well then don't play around with the camera. If you are after a full range of tones, don't play around with the camera (although this may be something of a generalization). However, even some simple adjustments in camera will start to manipulate the image in a creative and powerful way. You can communicate this look to the rest of the team via the monitor so the collaborative process is efficient and focused. This is very powerful. especially on tight budgets where departments may not have had all the time and resources to plan and communicate their ideas.

Film DoPs who are used to getting the look they want in post are amongst the strongest voices against HD. Some have said they would ban a big HD monitor on set. Other DoPs will realize that they may not always get to the grade, so shooting with an in-camera look gives more authorship than just shooting straight. If the director doesn't like the in-camera look, he or she can have their chance to say so during the shoot. However, beware of very strong looks where the image cannot be pulled back in post. This is a battle for creative control between the DoP, the post house and savvy directors with a background in Photoshop!

22   Can HD Cameras Handle Extremes of Temperatures and Humidity?

Video cameras love the cold as they have inbuilt 40 watt heaters. They are more susceptible to heat, but the crew are more likely to keel over before the camera fails. However, humidity is always an issue with tape-based recorders. There are humidity sensors that shut the camera down before the tape gets too sticky. A well-versed HD or video crew know what precautions to take in humid conditions.

23   "HD Post Is Complicated and Time-consuming"

A well set up HD production will compress a production schedule: trailers etc. can be extracted at any time; audio recorded along with the picture is a great feature for tight deadlines or low budgets; shooting 25p in Europe simplifies the post route.

24   "Audiences Think that HD is Awful"

There is no evidence to suggest that a cinema audience can even see a difference between film-originated material and HD-originated material transferred to film! The contrast ratio of projected film prints is the same, regardless of whether the image originated on 35 mm, HD or DV. However, it is becoming clear from the United States that audiences prefer digital projection to film projection. Multiplexes with digital projectors make more money.

25   What is a Viper?

A Viper is an HD camera head. That is, an HD camera without a built-in recorder. The Viper can output an HD signal to either an HD disc recorder or to an HD tape recorder. The Viper can also output a non-TV format-based HD picture, 4:4:4. On location, this signal is recorded on a hard disc or to HDCAMSR and is the highest quality HD picture available at the moment. Also the Viper is the only HD camera that can record full height (1080) lines cinemascope aspect ratio pictures. Note that the Sony f950 camera can also output 4:4:4.

26   What is 4:4:4?

It indicates that there has been no sampling of colours or luminance before recording. This equates to richer pictures and fewer artefacts, a very important improvement for bluescreen. However note that on the Sony HDCAMSR format a 4:4:4 image is compressed 4.2:1 during recording.

27   What is 720p?

720p is one of the many digital TV standards. The picture is made up of 1280×720 pixels with a frame rate of 60p. It is a transmission standard as well in the United States. Panasonic use this standard for their Varicam camcorder. Bear in mind that in the same way that HDCAM samples 1920×1080 pixels to 1440×1080, so does DVCPRO-HD compress 1280×720 to 960×720.

28   "HD Is Lower Resolution than 2K"

When most people talk of 2K they refer to a half 2K scan of an Academy frame. A 2K scan of Academy is actually 1828×1332. HD is usually 1920×1080.

29   Doesn't 3:1:1 or 4:2:2 Sampling Throw Away Lots of Important Colour Information?

Yes and no. Try this test. Connect a HD camera to a large monitor and look at the live picture. Record the scene. Replay and look at the scene off tape. Note the differences. Can you see any differences? Can you even see that the picture you are watching is a replay and not live? However, a computer will see a difference when you try to key. Not all compression is bad, but it does have the potential to bite. You cannot key an HD picture unless it was recorded on a hard disc. No doubt it is easier to key an HD picture from a uncompressed recording but test for yourself with a non-linear editing suite. Do this test at a couple of companies and at least one that does not have a telecine suite!

30   Are HD Viewfinders Awful?

Yes they certainly are. They display only half to two-thirds the resolution that the camera records. Although the black-and-white CRT tube is scanned at HD resolution it does not seem possible to cram any more phosphors into a 2 inch CRT tube. New displays will be released that promise full resolution colour pictures in a small package using new display technology.

31   "HD Cameras Make a Lot of Noise"

They are a little noisier than film cameras. Note that the internal fan on some camcorders can be programmed to switch itself off during a take.

32   "Digital Effects are Expensive"

Not all digital effects are expensive. Simple effects such as split screen, cloning, locked-off blue screen are low-cost effects in the HD environment. In fact these effects can be previewed and explored in an offline. For instance, bracketing exposure on a locked-off general view is a valuable tool to capture a contrasty scene. However, as a general rule if the camera moves then the cost of these simple effects can become prohibitive, especially to low budget productions. The director and DoP should have a clear idea before the shoot as to what is available in post-production.

33   "HD Cameras are Large and Heavy"

They can be configured with accessories that make them look like a Christmas tree! A camera 42 inches in length is possible. However, lower quality, lighter and smaller HD camcorders are available in a 20 inch package. Part of the size and weight is sometimes due to large, fast lenses.

34   Is there an HD Minicam?

HD minicams are slowly being introduced but there is a good range of box style cameras available.

35   What is HDV?

HDV is a new recording standard aimed at consumers. It uses DV style compression, to record a so called HD picture. The recording has less data than a normal DV recording and uses 60 to 1 compression.

36   What are Genesis, Dalsa, Kinetta and Arri D20 cameras?

These are new cameras that use large single chip sensors rather than using a prism and 3 sensors. This enables the use of existing 35 mm film lenses, which have reduced depth of field over current HD cameras. The Genesis uses a 12 million pixel CCD chip in the super 35 mm format, the Dalsa has a 8 million pixel CMOS sensor and the early prototype of the Arri D20 has a 6 million pixel CMOS sensor. The Kinetta designers hope to have interchangeable sensors and on board digital storage. The Genesis electronics are designed by Sony the mechanicals by Panavision, it utilises the Sony SRW1 portable tape recorder which can be removed from the camera.

Fig 2.7 The new Genesis HD film camera from Panavision

37 What is a Bayer filter?

A bayer filter is a colour filter array in a checkerboard pattern that is placed over a single chip ccd or cmos imager to create a colour image. 50% of the pixels are filtered green, 25% red, and 25% blue. Averaged together, a Bayer chip misses up to 67% of the colour information in the image. This isn't as bad as it sounds. Complex calculations from surrounding pixels are made to interpolate the missing colours at each pixel. However the actual detail is more difficult to "guess" and can result in artefacts or softness.

Bayer pattern colour cameras do not produce equivalent resolution to 3 chip sensors.

So a 4k or 2k Bayer chip may have 3k and 1.5k resolution respectively. This puts the resolution similar to or better than 1920×1080 4:2:2 or 4:4:4 recording. Careful testing of these cameras should be undertaken for blue or greenscreen applications.

38 Should I go "Native"?

There are many HD cameras, made for live TV that use with imagers that can only scan at 59.97i or 60i. Manufacturers add conversion boards to the base station or to the ccu to convert the frame rate from 59.97 or 60i to 24p, 30p or 720p. Technically speaking this is much less desirable than altering the scanning rate of the ccd or cmos. Native frame rate is the rate which the sensor is being scanned, which is not necessarily what is being output to a vtr.

"Native" is now also being loosely used in post-production to describe uncompressed images in "native codec" of HDCAM or DVCPROHD.

39   Can I Shoot in Cinemascope Aspect Ratio?

There are a number of ways to achieve a cinemascope aspect ratio image to the audience.

The Viper camera has a ccd structure that enables full 1920×1080 HD resolution in cinemascope aspect ratio using existing lenses. For other $2/3$ inch cameras with 16×9 aspect ratio ccds we can use a Canon relay lens that fits between lens and camera. This relays the 2.35:1 middle portion of the image only and optically "squashes" into the 16×9 sensor.

The third method is to crop the 16×9 image in post-production. This results in a drop in active lines from 1080 to 700. This was the method used in "Star Wars Attack of the Clones".

40   Should I use Film Curves and Cine Gamma Curves in the Camera if I am Transferring to Film?

It is not essential to use special gamma curves in the camera. The ccds themselves have a fixed dynamic range. Film curves allocate more in camera "processing" to highlights at the expense of other parts of the picture. It is far better to control the image through lighting and exposure. Small gains can be achieved if careful calibration between camera and post is orchestrated.

41   Does Apple's Final Cut ProHD Edit DVCPROHD in "Native" Mode?

If the image has been imported from the firewire output of the DVCPROHD VTR it exists in the computer, as it did on tape in "native" mode. One can perform a (cuts only) conform by using timecode and not having to uncompress the image. This then, is a "lossless" procedure. However, once a mix or any effect is undertaken the data has to be uncompressed and losses occur.

The Sony Xpri can import HDCAM images in "native" mode via a SDTI output on HDCAM VTRs.

42   Is HD Equipment Reliable?

Based on previous experience, a new camera, recording format or post-production tools are generally not bug free or fully developed when first sold.

43   What Are the Benefits of Shooting HD?

- Offers an alternative shooting regime in respect to stock costs.
- All takes are available in the edit.
- Confidence that the set can be struck.
- Creative collaboration on set between departments when using an HD monitor.
- Fast post-production route.
- No penalty for multiple takes, creative freedom of exploring performances.
- Generally faster lighting and shooting.
- Offers greater depth of field in low light situations.
- Technical problems can be caught on set quickly.
- Back-up camera can be used as second unit for the cost of a tape.

44   What are the Drawbacks of Shooting HD?

- Less contrast range than film.
- Less resolution than 35 mm film.
- New on-set disciplines need to be learnt.
- Minimum depth of field is greater than 35 mm film.
- Cables connected to camera.
- Restricted range of colours, different colour response than film.
- Back-up camera is expensive.
- Shortage of crews with HD experience.
- HD viewfinders are poor.
- Post-production routes are still being established.
- Conflicting advice, rapidly evolving equipment and software.

45   What is the Most Important Thing to Consider When Shooting HD?

The script.

3

HD Film Production in Scandinavia–Case Studies

3.1   Ingmar Bergman Meets Hi-Tech, *By Lasse Svanberg*

It looks simple when you read it. But I can promise you that it will be very trying. My demands on you will be very high. As high as the demands I put on myself in reaching the maximal expression. This is the absolutely last thing I do, I will never direct again. And when you say that, there is only one consideration, one loyalty that really counts–that towards the work itself.

(Ingmar Bergman, talking to actors and crew, 6 September 2002, two days before shooting commenced on *Saraband*)

Pre-production and Production

At the end of November 2002 I got a phone-call: 'Hi, it's Ingmar Bergman. The old one. I want to raise hell.' He wanted to discuss, in the manner of a sincere colleague, the sound problems he had encountered during his last film, *Saraband*. In fact, he wanted to have a row, but in such a way that other directors and producers would learn from his recent and hard-earned experiences of working with brand-new digital production tools. With this in mind I suggested a video interview, to be screened at the Nordic Film & TV Seminar (NFTV) in the Film House in Stockholm, this having been for 30 years the most important discussion forum and meeting place for Scandinavian film and TV professionals.

The interview took place in the Film House, 22 January 2003, in the smallest Film House cinema, named 'Julius' after our famous silent-film cinematographer, Julius Jaenzon. On the way up to the cinema, I took the opportunity to ask a few questions: 'Ingmar, I assume that you do not have a mobile telephone? – Never in my life! – Do you have a computer? – Are you crazy! – How then do you write your manuscripts? – By hand, of course. And then have them typed out.' It turned out that he had just ordered 4000 new pages of the manuscript writing pads (size A4, yellow with black lines) which he has always used since he started out as a filmmaker in Filmstaden,

Fig 3.1   Ingmar Bergman during the interview (photo: Leif Hedman)

Stockholm in the mid-1940s, which indicates that while, at the age of 85, he may end his filmmaking with *Saraband,* he is certainly not done with writing.

IB (as he is often called in Sweden) was in very good spirits, even better when he saw Jan-Hugo Norman behind one of the two DV cameras (he shot the documentary on the making of *The Magic Flute,* a costly SVT production in the Film House Studios in 1974). Our interview lasted an hour. An edited 20-minute version was shown at the NFTV seminar on 8 February, followed by a video statement from Philip Bennet, of Thomson-Grass Valley Group, and presentations from Torbjörn Ehrnvall, Assistant Director, and Per Sundin, Lighting Director, about their experiences from the *Saraband* production at SVT Studios.

Background

Saraband is not a sequel to *Scenes from a Marriage,* although it uses the same two leading characters, Johan (Erland Josephson) and Marianne (Liv Ullman). In the interview IB emphasized that it is a *chamber play,* originally written without having film, TV or stage theatre in mind. (The title is, by the way, the name of a very old and slow Spanish dance.) 'There are always two persons in the shot, confronted with each other and it is thus of *vital* importance that their voices can be heard properly, with all the nuances and shades of the human voice.' *Saraband* was, in other words, a studio-shoot with intimate dialogue scenes and many intense close-ups and tight two-shots.

It should be noted that IB is famous within the Swedish film production community for (among other things) his super-hearing, but only in his right ear. A volley of shots from a machine gun during his military service limited the hearing on his left side. It is hard to imagine a more demanding director than Ingmar Bergman when it comes to dialogue reproduction for cinema and TV.

Choice of Production Technique

In the middle of April 2002 IB was shown parallel tests of the same scene on HDTV and 35 mm film, and was astounded by the high quality of the HDTV images (Sony 25p HD CineAlta): 'I just couldn't by eye make out a difference!' HDTV had been suggested by the SVT production staff in order to secure for the future such an exclusive and expensive TV drama production, it being IB's last work for the TV and cinema screen, bringing to a close a lifetime of achievement embracing some 40 feature films and 13 TV drama productions. SVT made extensive tests with Sony HD cameras but realized after a while that the black-and-white viewfinders would not be good enough for this kind of demanding studio production. 24p HD Sony cameras were furthermore not intended for three-camera shoots.

The whole HDTV idea was scrapped during the summer, causing considerable anxiety in the production team. Then SVT's HDTV expert Lars Haglund gave the team a hint about a brand-new HDTV camera, Thomson 6000 Mark II, which could also be run progressively. The technical decision-makers went to Holland, became very impressed with what they saw, especially the effective colour viewfinders, crossed their nervous fingers and took the decision. At that time there existed only *five* such cameras in the world, and Swedish Television got four of them (three for production and one as back-up) through a package deal with Belgian facility house Alfa Cam, which also included a special OB van developed for the latest Football World Cup. A decision like that requires a considerable amount of courage – and a bit of luck.

SVT now felt ready to start the world's first three-camera, progressive HDTV drama shoot (which caused study visits from, among others, BBC Drama). The shooting was planned to go on from 18 September to 11 November 2002, mostly in SVT's largest studio, Studio 1. Torbjörn Ehrnvall had Ingmar's warning 'remember that I don't want *any* technical problems whatsoever, in such a case I go home' ringing in his ears. (IB had recently finished a radio theatre production where a digital mixer turned out to be an irritating and unreliable work-tool.)

Lots of tests were made before production began but it was forgotten to run the three HD cameras together for sound-tests. By ear the sound-level seemed to be the same as the three Philips cameras SVT had used on IB's TV drama *Bildmakarna* (The Picture Makers) successfully and less than a year ago. Thus the SVT technical team concentrated on achieving highest possible image quality.

Shooting Problems

The first day in the studio went smoothly since it involved wide shots in a large set-up. The second day however required work in a more confined studio space with a traditional three-camera set-up. And the result was disastrous. 'In my earphones I hear an undefined noise. *What the hell is this?*' yelled an irritated IB. A technical adviser assured him that it was nothing to worry about 'since we can filter it out'. This made IB suspicious, since he had heard these kind of excuses too many times before. 'If you filter out a disturbing background noise on the soundtrack, it also means that you remove something from the human voice, especially in the middle register.' He was then told that the 'noise-generator' was the built-in fans of the HD cameras, essential for cooling their advanced electronics. And IB blew his top! 'They have tricked us into using cameras with manufacturing defaults ... excellent for shooting *silent movies* with!'

The dailies from the second day were quickly delivered to Gabor Paszjor, in charge of post-production. 'Must we really *re-shoot?*' asked or rather pleaded Torbjörn Ehrnvall. Paszjor did not 'filter', he chose to digitally erase the electronic noise wherever there was silence. IB then listened but did not approve. He gave the team 48 hours to produce functioning camera blimps. The cameras were then wrapped in sound-absorbing material from a nearby, rebuilt sound studio, doubling their size. From now it was a *one-camera* production, although all three cameras could be used and be pre-placed in different set-up's, therefore making it quicker to move from one set-up to another, which, miraculously enough, meant that the original shooting schedule could be maintained to the end, and that the budget was not over-reached.

During the summer IB had worked out a detailed three-camera shooting script at his home on Fårö. He now showed his greatness as a director combined with solid practical experience as a producer. Very quickly he rewrote the production for one camera, which, incidentally, made the lighting director *Per Sundin* very happy.

During our interview IB recalled the 1940s in Filmstaden and muttered angrily that he never expected to encounter these kind of problems in the year 2003, at the end of his working life and having hired the most exclusive digital production tools of our time. 'In the 40s and 50s we worked mostly

Fig 3.2   Ingmar Bergman with blimped HD camera (photo: Bengt Wanselius)

with Debrie cameras. The material then used for sound-proofing was lead, which made the cameras extremely heavy. Still it was necessary to use big blankets over the cameras in order to cut out the camera noise. These damn blankets have followed me almost my whole life as a filmmaker. All the way from my first film in 1946 I have been raising hell about the sound. Until 1970.'

And what happened then? 'I met a very special guy named Owe Svensson. He was thinking in new ways. Claimed that the quality of the dialogue sound was entirely dependent on how the microphone was held and operated. An art in itself. A very special knowledge. Although he was First Sound Technician he chose to operate the boom himself on several of my films. In the Swedish feature films I've seen, and they're many, the sound quality is very uneven. Very good and distinct in two-shots, in wider shots it often gets a lot worse. Not to speak of television, where the sound is often disastrous.'

As examples of good, distinct dialogue sound he pointed to American and British films (having just re-screened *David Copperfield*). Aside from the sound problems on *Saraband,* IB was very happy with the image quality and was especially pleased to have found a young SVT Lighting Director, Per Sundin, who had learnt to 'set the lights in the same extraordinary way as Sven Nykvist'. He also thought it was pure joy to sit together with his old 'partisan' Sylvia Ingemarsson in the digital editing suite.

Fig 3.3 IB (with script on the left) during the shooting of *Hets* with a Debrie camera 1943 (photo: Svensk Filmindustri)

When our video interview was over he went over to DoP Jan-Hugo Norman, patted his small DV camera on the head and said, sort of to himself: 'Yes, yes, I know that this is where the future is.'

During the NFTV seminar the IB interview was followed by a short video recorded statement by Philip Bennett, responsible for HD cameras at Thomson-Grass Valley Group, who attended and lectured at the seminar but unfortunately had to leave before the IB interview was screened. Bennett was very well aware of the problems. 'An HDTV camera holds *five times as many electronic circuits* as a SDTV camera. The electronics require fan-cooling to prevent over-heating, just like in really powerful computers. Temporary, home-made blimps can, I'm afraid, increase the risk of over-heating. Thomson is, however, working hard on solving the problem. Lower the fan sound? Shut off fans automatically when recording starts? Better power management? Physically more robust camera bodies – which would add size and weight?' Ingmar Bergman's complaints had obviously reached him well ahead of the NFTV seminar.

This, by the way, was not the first time IB has taken bold technical production decisions. He decided that *The Magic Flute* (1975), a lavish studio production of Mozart's opera, should be shot on 16 mm Eastman Color. Standard 16 mm – a *very* controversial decision at the time. Not only did it work, however, it was a great success. Part of the explanation is that SVT at that time were world pioneers in scanning 16 mm colour negative to videotape in their newly developed A/B roll telecine.

Recording Techniques

Torbjörn Ehrnvall, with 30 years and 500 productions behind him at SVT, worked closely with IB as Assistant Director and also shared the technical responsibility with Producer Pia Ehrnvall, Ola Westman and Irene Wicklund, TOM (Technical Operations Manager). Recording on D-5 was considered but abandoned because of shortage of recorders. Sony HD-CAM recorders turned out to be a better choice. For the planned three-camera production they had geared up with seven VTRs in the AlfaCam OB van, three HD-CAMs, three DigiBetas and one DV. One of the advantages with the new Thomson 6000 camera is that it can deliver both a progressive HD signal and a 16:9 SDTV PAL signal simultaneously.

All involved on the studio floor (and in the OB van of course) became gloriously happy over the images they saw on the HD monitors. 'Why, why, why for heaven's sake can't these gorgeous images be shared with us by the

Fig 3.4 The only location shot in *Saraband*: HD camera on a four-wheel motorcycle (photo: Bengt Wanselius)

TV viewers!' they cried. And then, on second thoughts: 'Well, perhaps in a few years when we can broadcast in 720p.'

Focus and focus-pulling problems became apparent. Is the focus really in the eyes or on the nose-tip? The SVT crew quickly learned the special demands of HDTV when it comes to high-resolution rendition of props, costumes, set design and especially make-up. It certainly all shows! Their newly acquired knowledge on HD production was shared with the NFTV seminar attendees during a special workshop in the Film House Studio 7 on 9 February 2003.

The Lighting Director, Per Sundin, pointed out how profoundly understanding IB is when it comes to the limitations and possibilities in lighting. At an early stage they decided *not* to get stuck in the so-called 'video marsh'. Meaning that for reasons of comfort (or economics) decide to use as little light as possible and 'enhance' in the camera. It was decided to work with 'the whole contrast package' and within the camera's best range. This demanded lots of tungsten 10Ks and 5Ks; the smallest used was 800W (often the biggest on TV drama shoots). 'And I promise you that it will *show,* especially on the big cinema screen', stated Sundin with a certain pride in his voice, yet still having maintained a minimalistic Sven Nyqvist look.

Fig 3.5   Erland Josephson (Johan) and Liv Ullman (Marianne) in *Saraband* (photo: Bengt Wanselius)

Thus far in this chapter information has been retrieved from the IB interview and presentations at NFTV Seminar at The Film House. Let us now move forward.

Post-production

What follows is transcribed from a taped interview with Assistant Director Torbjörn Ehrnvall on 3 November 2003.

The final editing process went smoothly, although IB changed his mind at the end, wanted to re-edit after 'final cut', meaning that the film had to be remixed in April. This complicated the HD version since back-tracking was needed. Storm Productions in Copenhagen solved this by onlining for us in Sony's X-PRI editing system. It was not only a question of re-editing but also of adding new material. It worked well since they had all our original material on their hard discs, and it was not transferred in video format but as raw data, which meant that when we started colour correction we had, in principal, first-generation material to work with.

After IB had approved the final edit and mix he was especially pleased with the sound for TV transmission in stereo. We, however, never listened to the Dolby Surround version at this stage. *Saraband* will be delivered in many different formats, which we have had in the back of our minds all the way through production. DigiBeta 16:9 PAL, an HD 1.85:1 version, future DVD and 35 mm cinema releases, I-sound tracks for international editions, with and without subtitles etc. All these problems, except one, were sorted out at the beginning of November.

After a completed and approved DigiBeta version, our work with a 35 mm cinema release print started. At first we tried to use SVT's colour correction parameters at The Chimney Pot, transferring them on a hard disc, but it didn't work for the simple reason that HD is 1.85:1 and PAL 16:9 is 1.77:1. Format incompatibility. Shadow mask problems. Per Sundin's problem in colour correction was that the HD monitor image has a lot more gradation and colour depth than the DigiBeta 16:9 monitor image which IB looked at during editing. Gorgeous images on the HDTV monitor often looked like 'shit' in 16:9 PAL. Trying to convince IB that these visual imperfections could be dealt with at a later stage was not easy. Sometimes we had to impair the HDTV image a bit and improve the PAL 16:9 image accordingly in order to keep the director in good spirits.

We have for instance done a few radical encroachments in the DigiBeta version, let me give you an example. We worked with a few powerful bouncer lights with reflecting screens. It turned out that they gave the older actors glossy, moist, almost tearful eyes, which didn't always fit the dramaturgy so well. These reflections literally burned 'holes' in the eyes of some actors on DigiBeta, without being a problem on HD tapes. In certain close-ups on

DigiBeta we had to digitally reduce the size of these round reflections of light. Internally we named it the 'Sparkling Eyes Problem'.

The 35 mm Film Version

At the end of June we managed to print out the first reel (22 minutes, containing the film's audiovisually most complicated scenes) on The Chimney Pot's Arri Laser Printer. It didn't look right! The Chimney Pot brought experts here from Arri to upgrade their laser printer and the improvement was astonishing. We then did a new 35 mm print and the colourist at FilmTeknik decided, with the best of film intentions, to add a little bit of yellow. The reel, with Dolby SR sound, was delivered at the beginning of July to IB on Fårö, where he has had his own 35 mm home cinema for the past five decades.

IB's opinion was that close-ups worked quite well, wide shots were generally a bit out of focus, the print generally 'piss-yellow' and the sound 'completely useless' (he had screened in mono). 'Let's skip the whole idea of cinema release and consider this a total fiasco!'

Now, here comes an interesting phase. Per Sundin and I met Nils Melander, the colourist at FilmTeknik, and studied the 'yellow' print especially from a contrast range viewpoint. It turned out that the added yellow was bad for *resolution*. RGB is RGB and if you add a complementary colour like yellow it affects resolution. Per and I still thought that contrast range and colour depth could be improved, the most common problem when transferring standard video to film. But Nils exclaimed, 'For heaven's sake, there is no more to get out from my 35 mm negative!' And we said 'But there's obviously plenty more on our HD tape!'

So, back to The Chimney Pot. We started working with the *gamma curve*, which you can do in the Arri Laser Printer. Instead of the previously relatively steep curve we applied a more levelled curve, we even lifted the black level and, of course, removed the added yellow. Other than that, the same basic filtration. And we were amazed by the quality of the next 35 mm shoot-out! The resolution had now improved considerably. We showed it to Nils Melander, who has 40 years' experience as a 35 mm colourist, and asked him: 'How can you distinguish this from a print from a 35 mm negative?' 'There's an easy way for me to answer that,' he said, 'it is in 16:9 and not in 1.85:1, but other than that ... very difficult. Well, on a really big cinema screen it might be a bit easier for me.'

End of interview with Torbjörn Ehrnvall.

Conclusion

The road to a successful TV release, future HD and DVD versions and, above all, a 35 mm cinema release version was full of ups and downs for

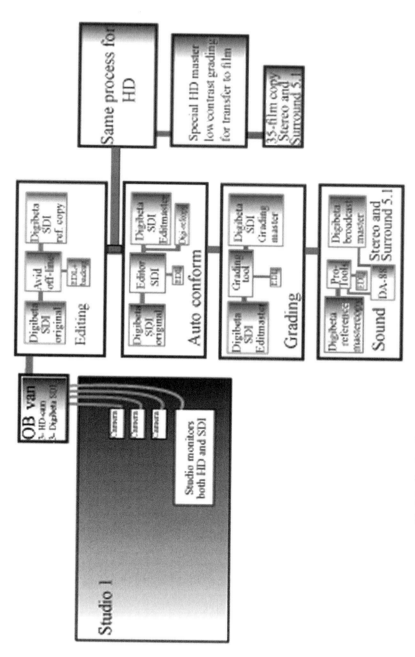

Fig 3.6 *Saraband* production flow scheme (courtesy Torbjörn Ehrnvall, SVT, 2004)

Saraband. In June 2002 the original idea of shooting on HDTV was totally discarded, but revived enthusiastically a month later, causing SVT a tremendous hi-tech rearmament at short notice. Camera noise problems brought the production to a complete halt after the second day of shooting – the second cause of real headaches within the production team. That was however solved due to good teamwork and an amazing flexibility from a then 84-year-old director. In July 2003 the director claimed that the idea of a 35 mm cinema release should be abandoned for technical quality reasons. That problem will be solved too, and as you have just read a colourist with 40 years' experience at a major 35 mm film lab had a hard time distinguishing the *Saraband* 35 mm cinema release version from a print made from a 35 mm camera negative.

Saraband got its grand TV premiere on SVT Channel 1 on 1 December 2003. On 3 December it was followed up by an excellent 47 minute behind-the-scene film from the production, *Direction: Bergman*, which should be shown by every film-school in the world with a serious ambition to educate film directors.

At the beginning of February 2004 *Saraband* was screened during the Film Festival in Dangères, France (as part of an Ingmar Bergman retrospective), for an audience of 1500 in a congress hall and as HD video projected on a 8×14 m screen. It was honoured by long, standing ovations.

HD video production techniques, both for film and TV, are today very well suited for sport, gala events or feature films with a lot of 'Bang! Bang!', pixel-pushing SFX action and post-sync. For low-voiced, intimate studio productions Thomson, Sony, Panasonic and others obviously still have some homework to do.

I can however almost promise that silent progressive HD 'film' cameras will be shown during IBC 2004 in Amsterdam. If it proves so, send a thought of thanks to Ingmar Bergman.

3.2   The Swedish Digital Experience, *by Lasse Svanberg*

The first feature film *entirely* shot with Sony 24/25p HD CineAlta cameras to get cinema release was not, as you might think, a George Lucas film. It was *Hem ljuva, hem* (Home, Sweet Home), produced by Sonet Film in Stockholm and released on 3 March 2001. The second was not a George Lucas film either, it was *Livvakterna* (Corporate Protection), also produced by Sonet Film and released 15 August the same year.

Twenty-six Swedish feature films were released in 2003. The list of shooting formats looks like this:

25p HD CineAlta	9
DigiBeta	2
DV-CAM	1
IMX 720p	1
35 mm film	7
Super 16 film	6

In other words, 50% of the national feature film output that year was shot not on film but on digital video media. (That figure can only be matched by Denmark in a current international perspective.) Why is that? And why was Sweden first to screen domestic HD feature films? Are we techno-freaks? Or just plain stupid, begging for 'arrows in our back'?

The answer can probably be found in the fact that Sweden (and other Scandinavian countries) have a long tradition of being so-called early adopters of new technology. History tells us that cinematographic industrial production in the longer fictional format moved north from France to Sweden and Denmark (which holds the oldest still functioning film production company in the world, Nordisk Film, founded in 1909). The early adopter concept also applies to the implementation of new technical inventions like telephony, colour TV, home video, home computers, broadband networks and mobile phones (with Finnish Nokia being the world leader) in Scandinavia – small, relatively wealthy countries with a hi-tech oriented population and industry.

A large country, like for instance France (Europe's biggest and oldest film producer), has bigger institutions, bigger companies, stronger unions, more powerful bureaucracies and also closer ties to traditional ways of making and showing films. The powers of inertia are lower in smaller countries and thus their ability higher to implement radical changes relatively quick. Size can be an obstacle to change (which certainly applies to present-day Hollywood). On the other hand, size also *dictates* the techno-economical conditions for large scale changes, as we will see when business model-based Digital Cinema gets it global roll-out in a few years' time.

Pioneering Work

Sweden's early entry on the HD 'film scene' should be credited to the young producer Joakim Hansson at Sonet Film, who at an early stage (2000) became convinced that digital was the way to go. Part of the background was that the most popular Swedish film in 2000, young Josef Fares' feature film debut *Jalla! Jalla!* (with some 900,000 tickets sold) was shot with small 3-chip DVCAMs (however without being a Dogma film).

Hansson wanted to go HD because he saw exciting opportunities to develop entirely new production methods, to increase creativity, save money and time and at the same time he was thrilled with the idea of doing pioneer work. Through persistence he managed to get hold of an early version of the Sony 24p HD HDW-F900 camera in mid-2000.

Home, Sweet Home was a low-budget film (0.9 million Euro) about a wife-beating husband with terrible outbursts of rage who gets 'killed' by his wife and young son but survives to live partly paralysed in a wheel-chair as a 'patient' in their home. It was a partly autobiographical story by young first-time director Dan Ying.

The HD camera arrived on a Friday evening and shooting started on the Monday. DoP Manne Lindwall struggled with the manual and made dozens of Help-type phone calls over the weekend. This minimal preparation and test period naturally meant several beginner's mistakes, like for instance choosing the setting ESC (without shutter) which created a typical 'video lag' but on the other hand gained 1.5 f-stops which came in handy on a semi-documentary style feature film. The film did fairly well in the cinemas, not least because of the marvellous performance by lead actor Michael Nyquist.

The early lessons learned from *Home, Sweet Home* led to the establishment of an 'HD troika' at Sonet Film – producer Joakim Hansson, director Anders Nilsson and DoP Per-Arne Svensson, with their first endeavour being *Corporate Protection* (2001), a 2 million Euro action film about organized crime in the Baltic region and part two of a trilogy starring the charismatic Jacob Eklund as police officer Johan Falk. The film became a box-office success (later also a hit on the VHS and DVD rental and sales market). Large parts of the film take place at night and in rain and the team was especially pleased with how well the F-900 HD cameras managed the deep blacks.

The Third Wave

The third and last part of the trilogy, *Tredje Vågen* (The Third Wave) was produced in 2003 with a budget of 3.9 million Euro (2.5 times a normal Swedish feature film budget). It involved 60 shooting days, European locations, lots of digital special effects and pyrotechnics. In September 2003 (during post-production of *The Third Wave*) I made an interview with the Sonet Film 'troika', trying to sum up their HD experiences.

'We had to learn this new technology from scratch, from the very beginning, like those pioneer filmmakers in the beginning of the last century,' said Joakim Hansson. Quite a challenge. Anders Nilsson added that the title *The Third Wave* has a double-meaning in a sense. The first wave of change was sound film, the second was colour and wide screen films and we are now experiencing the third wave – digital filmmaking. Both Joakim and Anders see mostly advantages in this transition. DoP Per-Arne Svensson agreed, but sighed while saying: 'I have just realized that at the end of this production I will have spent almost as much time at the digital post house (The Chimney Pot) as I did behind the camera on the set.' This is a new aspect of DoP work which, as I see it, has not been discussed properly. Svensson emphasized how important it is today for DoPs to learn how to master 'the digital dark-room', whether they shoot on film or digitally.

How has their HD work improved, I asked them, compared to a couple of years ago? Large HD monitor on the set (re-calibrated as soon as it has been moved), Zeiss Prime HD lenses (no zoom lenses), two-camera shoot and Zeiss collimator for back-focus checking on the set. On *Corporate Protection* they were more nervous about the back-focus problem and used ND filters and stopped down a few stops for this reason. Most of *The Third Wave* is however shot wide open. Zeiss Primes are made for that.

P.A. Svensson prefers to use a neutral menu setting trying to capture as much image information as possible and then create the visual look of the film in digital post-production. This working method however, demands that there is enough in the budget to allow the DoP to spend weeks (not 5 or 6 days) in digital post. If it is desired to have the special 'look' visible on the set it is quite easy to program the large HD monitor via a memory card and then switch quickly between the look and 'neutral'. There are, however, situations where a standard menu setting should not be used, for instance when filming snow scenes in bright sunlight or on really dark night shots. He strongly recommends (a) to use F-900 upgrade #3 with improved menu setting possibilities and much more detail in highlights, and (b) to develop

Fig 3.7   Riot scene in *The Third Wave,* shot in Munich (photo: Sonet Film)

a really close and trustful relationship with the person you are going to work with in the post house.

'There has been tremendous progress in the post-production process the last year, almost on a weekly basis,' said Anders Nilsson. 'Now I feel, for the first time, that I have more or less total creative control as a director and can do exactly what I want. We directors have now been blessed with the same creative freedom as the music makers got through their new digital work tools some ten years ago. We are not working with film cameras anymore, we work with *computers!*'

He gave several examples of this new creative freedom in the digital editing suite. 'I would like to have some more smoke in this scene ... No, no, that's too much ... That's it!' Click, click, click and it's done. In real time. 'Can you put a small gleam in Jakob's left eye? I want him to look a little bit more *dangerous* in this close-up.' Click, click, click and it's done.

I asked Anders if he can conceive of going back to shooting on film. 'No, no, it would feel like going from a word processor back to a manual typewriter.'

The Infrastructure

Getting an early start means that there has been time to learn from mistakes, gradually refine the production machinery and build up an infrastructure consisting of equipment suppliers, film lab and post house know-how and, not least, personal knowledge and experience of directors, producers, DoPs, editors and post-production managers. This gradual transition from film-based to digital production methods has, of course, been a bit controversial and not loved by all. Folkets Hus Digital Houses (see Chapter 7) should be included in the Swedish Digital Cinema infrastructure, although this pioneering E-cinema network is still too small to create economy of scale benefits (eight screens at the end of 2003). Still it has functioned as an important test bed for evaluating digitally produced feature films on big cinema screens, as 35 mm release prints, digital film prints (LTO data cartridges) and as projected HD-CAM video tapes.

Conclusion

Industry experts I have talked to predict that the number of digitally produced feature films in Sweden will drop from 50 to approximately 30% during 2004, the reason being that a few new users of HD 24p video production technology have become disappointed (especially with the cost savings aspects) and will therefore go back to film. It has also become evident that if you produce a 'traditional' feature film with professional actors, a rigid shooting script and low shooting ratios (1:10–15) there is not very much to be gained from going digital in the production phase. The experiences from *Mamma, Pappa, Barn* (Kjell-Åke Andersson, 2003) shot on Sony IMX 720p were, however, very positive. It looked quite good on the cinema screen and cost considerably less than HD 24p. It will probably be a route followed by others.

I am convinced that directors, producers and DoPs will gradually learn how to fully exploit the specific advantages of digital film production – instead of trying to produce 'typical 35 mm films' on HD video and give them a 'film look'. Out of that will sooner or later come exciting, creative films that could *not* have been made on film in the traditional way and which do *not* look like film. To follow this trend, for good and for worse, there are good reasons to turn your attention to Sweden and Denmark, because of the simple fact that they have the longest continuous experience of HD film production in Europe. Danish director Lars von Trier has, for instance, come a long way in establishing specific 'HD aesthetics' (see the following chapter, The Danish Digital Experience). Cheap and easy-to-use digital work tools like the Desktop Movie concept will further accelerate this process on a worldwide basis.

3.3   The Danish Digital Experience, *By Jens Ulff-Møller*

Video is good, film is bad.

(Lars von Trier in a private interview with David Nielsen-Ourø)

The most successful Danish movies in recent years have all been digital productions.[1] The filmmakers connected to the Zentropa Company in particular have spearheaded the exploration of digital film production, which began with Thomas Vinterberg's movie *The Celebration,* shot by Anthony Dod

---

[1]Digitally produced Dogma movies: Thomas Vinterberg, *The Celebration* (1998); Lars von Trier, *The Idiots* (1998); Lone Scherfig, *Italian for Beginners* (2000) cinematography Jørgen Johansson; Åke Sandgren and Jørgen Johansson, *Truly Human,* (2001); Ole Christian Madsen, *Kira's Reason* (2001); Susanne Bier, *Open Hearts* (2002); Natasha Arthy, *Old, New, Borrowed, and Blue* (2003).

Other digital movies shot on DigiBeta: Lars von Trier, *Dancer in the* Dark (2000); Per Fly, *The Bench* (2000), *The Inheritance* (2003); Annette K. Olesen, *Minor Mishaps* (2002).

HD movies: Lars von Trier and Anthony Dod Mantle, Peter Hjorth, *Dogville* (2003); Lone Scherfig, Jørgen Johansson, *Wilbur wants to Kill Himself* (2002); Marlene Vilstrup, *Zafir* (2003). In production: Susanne Bier, Morten Søborg, *Brothers*; Thomas Vinterberg, *Dear Wendy*; Lars von Trier, *Manderlay*.

Mantle with Sony's first mini-DV camera in 1998. Then came films such as *The Idiots, Italian for Beginners, The Bench, The Inheritance* and *Dancer in the Dark*. Recent films shot in HD include: Lars von Trier's Dogville (2003), Lone Scherfig's *Wilbur wants to Kill Himself* (2002) and Marlene Vilstrup's children's film *Zafir* (2003), Susanne Bier's *Brothers,* Thomas Vinterberg's *Dear Wendy* (2004) and Lars von Trier's latest movie, *Manderlay*.

So, is the success of Danish movies a result of digital production? What specifically are the advantages and disadvantages of HD production? For comments on this I have interviewed the digital cinematographer Jørgen Johansson (*Wilbur*), and Zentropa's technical wizard Peter Hjorth (*Dogville*).

Digital shooting is not in itself a recipe for success, according to Jørgen Johansson. But, digitalization has had as result that the technicalities have stepped into the background, and therefore we have been able to focus on producing more interesting movies. 'We have been able to put aside stiff, old, heavy methods of producing movies, and instead we have been able to have our fling when shooting digitally: shooting is not so costly, so we have more resources, which has released energy, and that is apparent for the spectators of the movies.'

Technical Issues: HD Image vs. 35 mm

'When you choose to shoot on HD rather than Betacam, the reason is that you want to obtain a real "film look", at least I consider HD image on Sony's 24p camera to be fairly close to 35', Johansson admits. He feels the HD image is indisputably the best image you can get, but it comes with serious technical disadvantages. It is extremely difficult to adjust the camera correctly, because you can adjust almost everything. And, since the adjustments are complicated, you may want to have an electrical engineer assisting with the operation of the camera on the set. It is necessary to "hit" correctly when shooting, because tolerances are small, with the result that correction in post-production is almost a non-existent option. Nobody really knows in depth what is going on inside the camera. At the moment there are no standards for settings that prescribe how to adjust the camera nor the projected image. (It is however, possible to set up the camera to an equivalent film stock setting and store this on a memory card.) On the other hand, the advantage of digital movies is that the projection is scratch free, with no flickering or jumping images.

Johansson and Hjorth agree that there are a lot of initial technical and aesthetic problems with HD shooting and digital projection, as there is with all new technology, but most problems are being solved little by little. And it is fascinating to be a pioneer, and take part in the development of a new technology that inevitably will become the universal method of filmmaking in the future.

Recording Format

Many filmmakers think that the quality of digital image is inferior to the celluloid image, and that movies shot on 35 mm look much better than the electronic image. But in reality, the preference for 35 mm seems to be psychological rather than based on technical advantages. We are so accustomed to the technical characteristics that the celluloid film stock dictates, that we are hardly aware of its aesthetic deficiencies. At present, digital shots provide a virtually different aesthetic, which has its specific technical problems and advantages. Film directors and cinematographers should therefore be aware of these characteristics and know how to take advantage of them before choosing the medium on which to shoot.

But the preference for film is based on something psychological. 'It is very strange, when you have worked with HD for some time and return to celluloid,' Peter Hjorth states. 'The excess quality of the film stock is actually not as large as you imagined. You still have to get it right when shooting on film. Film is better, but it is not so much better as one might imagine. It has to do with what you are accustomed to, or how the spectator is brought up.'

The resolution in digital images is better with HD, but it can still be improved. The image capture format is 1920 pixels horizontally and 1080 pixels vertically, but at the moment the image is down-sampled to 1440 horizontal and 1080 vertical pixels before compression in 16:9, 1.77:1 or masked to Cinemascope format and the compression can be problematic. Normal film copies have about 2000 lines even though there were 4000 to 8000 in the negative, so the quality of a celluloid movie normally does compare to the HD quality. 'The problem with HD is that there is no headroom in the recording format, as there is on celluloid. Therefore, shooting has to be more precise. When editing a film you can zoom into the negative, or copy a second time, but such photographic manipulations are rarely possible on HD. You have to have optimal shots, in order to obtain OK copies, but at the moment, there is no excess as in celluloid, as we are accustomed to, one cannot obtain extra data from the negative, as in celluloid,' Peter Hjorth states.

The compression also results in a shallow black – white exposure room. There are few details in the black, as well as in the white, which tends to become burnt-out white areas, much more than in other digital recording media. The compression of HD images means that the quality becomes progressively worse for each generation. Sony has come out with a HD-CAM SR, which uses a lower compression ratio, and Thomson's Viper camera interfaces directly with an uncompressed hard disc system capable of recording full colour RGB, thereby bypassing the limitations of storage on digital tapes.

Another problem is the *depth of field*. HD cameras have short focal lengths and therefore a deep focus, which is well suited for the newscasts and documentaries for which the cameras were created. But a deep focus is not ideal for shooting fiction films, in which the main character should be isolated from the background. The effect of deep focus is that the background becomes more important and can interfere in the picture, which becomes cluttered with unimportant details. By focusing on different elements in the picture, the cinematographer directs the attention of the spectator from one element in the image to another. But since important features in the foreground cannot be isolated from the background, then the digital image can look 'messy'. A way to overcome the deep focus problem is to shoot in controlled studio surroundings, or to shoot long shots on location. Arriflex, the traditional film camera provider, is in the process of designing a digital fiction camera with traditional focal lengths from film cameras, which will solve the deep focus problem. It is expected to hit the market in a couple of years.

The aspect ratio 1:1.77 expands the image compared to the Academy format (3:4), which the Dogma rules prescribed. 'It has the breadth, which functions well even in a psychological film, such as *Wilbur,*' Lone Scherfig explains, 'because more people can be together in the image, so that you don't have to cut from person to person. There is space for them, so you can make a shot in which more people are together. When two actors are together, it is possible to shoot almost a close-up of both actors. You can obtain serenity if you are aiming at that' (*Wilbur,* DVD commentary).

The Japanese have overcome the problem of the lack of pixels with a 4K digital camera, but still the black–white room appears to be narrow. The company, Communications Research Laboratory showed a test film programme in Paris in December 2003 in a stunning quality, which by far exceeded that of conventional movies in the richness of details. The test film *Fall in Kyoto* had a poetic atmosphere in red and yellow colours of falling leaves with stunning details. The same location appears in *Lost in Translation* but in a significantly lower image quality than the 4K camera was able to produce. The recording format however, required some kind of compression, which had a negative effect on the black – white balance. The test films were shot at 24 fps, which was too slow to reproduce the movements of a Japanese dancer, whose arms seemed at times to disappear. Still, the 4K projection demonstrated clearly that the future belongs to digital projection.

Other problems arise when the digital movie is transferred to celluloid for distribution, which has to be done because we do not yet have digital exhibition in Denmark. 'The movies that come out on HD today look great. The image is sharp, lush, and with a good contrast. But when the digital master is transferred to a celluloid premiere copy, you have to make an optimal transfer with equipment that can rarely be adjusted to anything but the specified factory adjustment in order to create an optimal copy,' Peter Hjorth states. 'In comparison, if you transfer from a 35 mm negative, the amount of information that you transfer to the premiere copy is only a fraction of the information present in the negative.'

Finally, it is necessary to introduce standard adjustments for the *projectors* in digital exhibition, such as using a standard speed, how to handle the adjustment of the colour balance, etc. 'It is currently necessary to make a copy for the average digital cinema. The parameters can vary on the projectors, and adjustments can become an endless process, so it would be preferable if we introduce a common standard,' Peter Hjorth states. 'That would take place in the distribution, which is even more uncontrollable than the production sector … not to mention the specific interests Hollywood might have in postponing the introduction of digital competition.'

'In fact, there is nothing fundamentally wrong with digital equipment. There are a lot of technical problems, because we are in a transition phase, but the problems are being solved. Many reject the HD format, claiming that something is wrong with the cameras, when in fact they are caused by economic problems, such as a budget too low to acquire sufficient light, or good actors, etc.,' Peter Hjorth explains.

Danish Digital Movies

The innovation of Danish filmmaking originated in a convergence between traditional film techniques and TV production, which has broken down stiff production patterns in filmmaking. In 1992 Danish Television invited Lars von Trier to direct the TV series *The Kingdom I* (1994), shot on 16 mm. The less rigorous TV production methods provided the foundation for the Dogme95 style. Lars von Trier first used digital cameras in the TV series *The Kingdom II* (*Riget II,* 1997). Danish Television continued to be of great importance for developing Danish cinema by employing young directors and cinematographers for the production of TV series, such as *Rejseholdet, TAXA,* Ole Christian Madsen's *The Spider* (2000), *Nicolaj and Julie* (2003), and most lately *The Chronicle* (*Krøniken,* 2003).

Digital movie production began with the first Dogma (Dogme95) movie, Thomas Vinterberg's *The Celebration,* prize-winner at Cannes in 1998. Even though the technical quality was poor, as it was shot with the first generation Sony mini-DV camera, the movie created euphoria among independent directors, Judy Irola explains: digital filmmaking was now possible – there was no going back to studio-controlled 35 mm filmmaking (Power to the Pixel, Channel 4). It is, however, the new Sony HD cameras that have first made it possible to obtain an image quality comparable with 35 mm celluloid film.

Dogville

Zentropa purchased HD cameras in order to enable Lars von Trier to shoot the movie *Dogville.* The story concerns the beautiful Grace (Nicole Kidman), seeking shelter in a village in the Rocky Mountains in the 1930s from a team of gangsters. In return Grace agrees to work for them. Slowly, the people of Dogville turn against her, and hand her over to the gangsters. Somebody coming from the outside trying to do good can be a provocation.

Lars von Trier is the film director who most systematically has embraced the new digital technology. Digital cameras with their 40–60 minute recording time had a profound effect on his way of handling the actors, because they could play and stay in character throughout the recording time. Furthermore, since the digital cameras are lighter, von Trier was able to shoot with the camera himself throughout the recording time, lasting up to one hour at a time.

Von Trier developed a new point-and-shoot aesthetics based on the hand-held camera he operated himself, in which he could interact with the actors while directing and shooting; the plot and the actors became the centre of action, rather than technical requirements or aesthetic considerations. In his Dogma movie *The Idiots* he began to operate the camera himself, while directing the actors at the same time, and he carried on this camera work in *Dancer in the Dark* (2000), and in *Dogville* (2003), in which he shot the main part of the movie himself with an Easyrig mounted HD camera.

Fig 3.8   Director Lars von Trier with an HD camera during shooting of his film *Dogville* (2003) (photo: Rolf von Konow)

Von Trier has developed a specific shooting strategy that enables him to find the essence in the characters and the stories, which arises out of necessity; beauty comes from necessity, a notion inspired from Wim Wender's *Light over Water,* and *Alice in den Städten.* So when von Trier shoots, there are no rehearsals, he starts filming right away, thereby enabling the actors to give their input. In the second takes von Trier will suggest changes. His aim is not to be restricted by the preparation, although he knows where a scene starts and where it has to get to.

Von Trier has realized that there is a philosophical difference between framing a shot and pointing the camera at something. 'When I point at what I want to see, I experience the feelings of the people in the frame much more strongly than whenever the camera moves to compose something superficial. When you aim, you consider the action in the middle of the image; when framing you consider how to place the image aesthetically within the frame, which takes away some of the energy in the image and the acting.' Lars von Trier reserves framing to establishing shots, where the use of the frame emphasizes the aesthetics of the image, he explains in the DVD commentary, to *Dogville.* 'I use the camera to see what I want to see. It's not framing, but using the camera as a way to see things, the way you use your eyes' (*Dogville*, DVD commentary).

With digitalization, a convergence between filmmaking and theatrical production has emerged. Von Trier explains that he tries not to frame, because 'when you frame, you are removing yourself from the content, as opposed to embodying yourself. ... It is *Verfremdung*' – a notion he inherited from Bertolt Brecht's theatre. 'When you *frame* something, you keep something out. When framing you obtain something peacefully that you want in the image. But this peacefulness is something that is nice to look at, but always weakens the content.' When commenting on Anthony Dod Mantle's long shots at a 45-degree high angle, Lars von Trier stated, 'you notice straight away that the actor becomes less important. In a composition, as soon as you know that a background fits right, you put a kind of layer – in between.' That's why von Trier likes the old Academy format, because it is difficult to frame the shots in it. 'The drama get stronger when you don't balance the pictures. It is very easy to make something well balanced.'

Dogville was shot with Sony's 24p HD camera, but with 25 frames per second, since all the other electronic equipment used to produce the movie was calibrated at that higher speed. The difference in speed between film and music created some problems in the post-production phase.

There are three kinds of shots in *Dogville.* First von Trier shot the close-up shots himself with a hand-held HD digital camera. Second, Anthony Dod Mantle shot the 45-degree crane, long shots with the same camera. Finally, Peter Hjorth shot the trick film from above with 13 DV cameras, which he moved around to a total of 156 locations, and then he combined the shots into one single image. The trick film is a further development of the 100-camera concept von Trier used in the musical and dancing sequences in *Dancer in the Dark*. Peter Hjorth also arranged the chroma-keyed shots of the dog, and of Nicole Kidman seen through the tarpaulin at the back of the truck, which has become one of the icons of the movie.

Von Trier explains that digital filmmaking provides access to many tools that were not always available in film. 'Having achieved this amazing modern world of digital technology, digital films are still very timid in their exploration of what it is possible to do; one can create layers and multi-layers of images.' The chroma-keyed images and the trick films clearly point to some of the little explored advantages of the convergence with television techniques, and demonstrate the superior qualities of digital montage, especially compared to the double exposure ghost scenes in Lars von Trier's TV series, *The Kingdom*.

Wilbur Wants to Commit Suicide

This film by Lone Scherfig was the first Danish HD file to appear in the movie houses. It is a story about two brothers who inherit an antiquarian bookstore in Glasgow. The oldest, Harbour, tries to take care of his suicidal brother, Wilbur. One day Alice, a cleaning lady at a hospital, and her daughter enter the shop. Harbour falls in love with Alice and marries her. When he dies from a terminal illness, Wilbur has to face reality, having to take care of Alice, her daughter, the bookstore and his own life.

Jørgen Johansson states: 'The film is shot on location in Glasgow as well as in the Zentropa studios outside Copenhagen. The idea was to shoot *Wilbur* in 'Scope on 35 mm, but it was the economics that forced us to work digitally. We were allowed to use Zentropa's new HD camera, when Lars had finished shooting *Dogville*. Jørgen Johansson would have liked to shoot on 35 mm, because the images look better on "real" film, but when choosing HD, you obtain an image that resembles film the most.

'A huge advantage was the monitor image you obtain from drawing a cable from the camera to a monitor, which the director can observe. In *Wilbur* we had a 64 kilo monitor with a fairly big image of unheard-of quality, and it was a huge advantage when discussing what was or was not in the picture. You just look at the monitor – it shows what you've got! The disadvantage was shooting on location in the streets of Glasgow, where a heavy monitor is not very practical.

'*Wilbur* was shot as a conventional feature film. We did not shoot a lot of footage. It was small, short takes – one to two minutes. We chose HD for economic reasons; it was not an artistic choice. On the other hand, it is also great to be up in front with the new technology. And I do not doubt for one second that within a limited number of years, all movies will be created digitally.'

Zafir

Zafir is a children's film about a young girl's dream of horses and friendship. The 11-year-old Anna owns the untameable Zafir until Sharbat comes, and they become friends due to their mutual love for Zafir. 'If the film had not been shot on HD it would have been made on Digibeta, and we would have had to accept a grainy image of the black horse on a grey day. HD clearly improved the film,' Peter Hjorth explains.

Brothers

Susanne Bier's upcoming movie, which is shot by Morten Søborg, is about Michael (Ulrik Thomsen). He has a wife, family and a career as commander of a special unit, which is sent to the war in Afghanistan. His younger brother Jannik (Nikolaj Lie Kaas) is just out of prison when Michael is reported killed in Afghanistan. Jannik offers to help Michael's wife, Sarah (Connie Nielsen) with the children. Slowly, Jannik and Sarah fall in love, and when Michael is found alive and returns, none of them can handle their former roles in life.

Morten Søborg explains that not only does the HD camera produce a much better image than DigiBeta, where half of the image information is thrown away in post-production, but in this movie they use progressional scan, in which all lines are scanned at the same time, which also helped to improve the quality of the image.

Morten Søborg, too, finds that the adjustments of the HD camera is complicated, which means that it is difficult to find the optimal setting. Furthermore, the heat of the camera influenced the back-focus, so that the camera could go out of focus if the temperature changed. In addition, the fan was noisy and could interfere with the sound recording, and the camera was mechanically unstable.

Morten Søborg finds that HD is still not the successor of 35 mm, though he admits that their camera was the first model to become available, and now lighter and more light-sensitive cameras have appeared. He has also experience with the new IMX format (720p) from shooting the Swedish feature film *Mamma, Pappa, Barn*.

Dear Wendy

Thomas Vinterberg's movie is about an 18-year-old outsider, Dick, a pacifist who lives in a poor mining town in the Midwest. One day he finds a small gun, which he names Wendy. It draws him into the town's gang of misfits, the Dandies. The group gives them strength and a sense of identity, not least as a result of their personally named weapons, which they have sworn never to use. But the rules are broken, when greater and more important principles are at stake.

Manderlay

Lars von Trier started shooting this movie in March 2004. Grace has arrived at a large plantation, Manderlay, in the South. The workers are more or less slaves, which Grace finds inhuman. The movie will be the second in Lars von Trier's USA Trilogy.

Conclusion

The success of Danish filmmakers suggests that the future is digital and that the initial problems are being solved. The success of Danish movies is to a large extent a result of embracing digital filmmaking, whether on DV, Betacam or HD. Lars von Trier, Europe's foremost film director, has summed up the positive experience with digital cameras, despite their technical deficiencies, laconically: 'Video is good, film is bad.'

Other digital movies shot on DigiBeta: Lars von Trier, *Dancer in the Dark* (2000); Per Fly, *The Bench* (2000), *The Inheritance* (2003); Annette K. Olesen, *Minor Mishaps* (2002).

HD movies: Lars von Trier and Anthony Dod Mantle, Peter Hjorth, *Dogville* (2003); Lone Scherfig, Jørgen Johansson, *Wilbur wants to Kill Himself* (2002); Marlene Vilstrup, *Zafir* (2003). In production: Susanne Bier, Morten Søborg, *Brothers*; Thomas Vinterberg, *Dear Wendy*; Lars von Trier, *Manderlay*.

3.4   A Finnish HD Experience–Hymypoika (Young Gods),
By Jarkko T. Laine

Pre-production

Hymypoika is a story about four young men in Helsinki, one of them carrying a camcorder wherever he goes, trying to capture moments of beauty and truth. They decide to start a club where every member must bring a videotape of their latest sexual adventure to the meetings.

I got involved in the production at quite an early stage, in October 2002 (five months ahead of shooting). I soon got a feeling that the shooting format had been decided a long time ago. The production company, Helsinki-Filmi, is a brand new one established by three young producers and this would be their first screen release feature. They were after a totally new and fresh approach to film making and wanted to become the pioneers of HD feature film making in Finland: 'True, realistic present day low-budget feature films.' The initial budget was one million Euro. The average age of the crew was 30.

In my opinion this would have been a perfect movie for Super 16 – lots of hand-held, two-camera shoot, many night exteriors and amateur actors (having *Fucking Åmål* in the back of my head). However, I lost my vigorous battle for film, but (as you will see later) became 'converted' during the post-production phase.

Production

Cameras

We chose Sony HD 24p CineAlta (at 25p), two Sony HDW-900 cameras fitted with Canon 'filmstyle' HD zoom lenses HJ 11×4, rented from P. Mutasen Elokuvakonepaja Oy in Helsinki. They were delivered only a few days prior to shooting which, however, gave us the necessary testing time. There was no ready-made camera location-package available at that time and the first two weeks were spent trying to put one together. We tried to modify some Super 16 equipment to fit HD, which took a lot of time and effort at the rental house. Since HD cameras are noisy (even on exterior shots), cumbersome soft-blimps had to be custom-made, which made hand-held shooting more difficult than it usually is.

The whole camera package became very heavy, some 18 kilos in the end. The weight was increased by an on-board monitor, Miranda down-converter, matte box, double batteries, lead blimp and cabling. Such a 'monster' is not very well balanced or even intended for hand-held shooting. Something must be done about the power supply! And the noise problem. Couldn't the cooling fans stop when the video drum starts to roll? And why can't the cassette door be tight? Is it made loose for extra cooling?

Some Other Practical Problems

Next time I will insist on a HD SDI on-board monitor. Now we had only a PAL on-board monitor. Nothing on HD should be judged from any form of PAL source. Only top quality HD monitors (which are very expensive) will do.

The HD monitor on the set was naturally occupied by the director and continuity. From a small SDI monitor I could tentatively judge exposure, without the need to run back and forth to the main rack of monitors, over that 'sea' of cables. I would also opt for HD SDI cabling which carries the signal through one cable only. In our case there were three more! Since we wanted to record all the shots on DVCAM (mainly for continuity, to check things quickly and save the master HD tapes), the signal needed to be down-converted to PAL on location. That created an enormous problem with cables, keep in mind, from two cameras. When doing long hand-held takes we unplugged most of the cables and sent the images to the director in wireless mode to his tiny DVCAM. He was very understanding and patient on these issues.

Two-camera shooting? I opposed it prior to the start of production but the director wanted to raise the chances of approved first takes as high as possible, considering that the leading actors were young and inexperienced. I became convinced, but it did make lighting and *mis-en-scènes* a lot more complicated. I did not envy my B-camera operator since he had a thankless mission on this hectic semi-docu style picture. For that reason he was sent out to do second unit work once in a while.

Focus Problems

During the first weeks of shooting it became more and more important for me to see my work on a bigger HD monitor or on a big silver screen. We were extremely worried about focus problems, since we shot wide open (f/2) most of the time and in very low light conditions. We were also dealing with young actors with very little (or no) acting experience, who quite naturally would have problems with hitting focus marks or even remembering their existence. When you shoot with prime lenses on film you can trust your 'gut' feeling in terms of focus, but on HD, with that inferior black-and-white viewfinder, you must make extra takes to be really sure that you have got it in focus. An additional challenge to me and my focus-puller was that our director, Jukka-Pekka Siili, is a 'one-or-two-takes' guy. After one good take he wanted to move further, which in a sense is reasonable on a tight schedule (we had 30 shooting days all together). However, when improvising with amateur actors and shooting wide open in low lighting conditions, you must allow for three or even four takes before moving on. Just before a take started I usually ran to the actors and whispered 'don't forget the focus marks' – it helped! Generally speaking, focusing is a crucial problem on HD, in comparison to film (even Super 16).

How about back-focus, the almost legendary 'HD fuzz'? This was a small problem for us; it did not roam and was only checked properly once a day (plus some quick additional checks before especially important scenes).

I hate the idea of having such a technical insecurity problem on the set and I would plead with camera manufacturers to attend to it in a sustainable way in future camera models.

I will definitely shoot the next HD film with DigiPrimes (or similar alternatives). Our Canon zooms were not sharp enough and are more or less unusable at the longest end in terms of resolution plus losing one f-stop. They are fine for TV work but not for HD feature film production.

Screening of Rushes

Rushes were screened once a week at the Generator Post, the first three weeks in the Spirit grading suite, later screen-projected (from master tapes) because renting the suite turned out to be too costly. I obviously wanted to screen rushes more frequently, but this was what we could afford budget-wise. When playing back HDCAM tapes a staff member had to assist and guard our tapes (our 'negative'), which was a bit impractical. We furthermore shot with two cameras all the time. During production I did not have the time to see all B-camera rushes, but I had a well trusted colleague and friend operating it.

I was quite surprised by how few were attending screenings. Since the crew thought they had already 'seen' the rushes on the location monitor, they were not that keen on seeing them again. I personally recommend daily screenings together with not only director, producer and DoP, but also set designer, sound engineer and costume designer, like in any other feature filmmaking process. It is an excellent opportunity to discuss were we stand at the moment. It is extra important on HD (or any) shoots with tight schedules where there is not enough time to talk on the set. Next time I do an HD picture I will strongly recommend sufficient budgeting and proper time-slots for frequent screenings of rushes.

Exposure

My experiences of shooting video (and I have done lots of it) were mostly DigiBeta-based before this production. That's where my approach to exposing images came from. (I had, however, never seen my DigiBeta images on the silver screen.) I used all my knowledge gained from the DigiBeta days and followed those principles. The only significant difference was that I realized that I cannot overexpose at all. Everything after one stop over becomes totally white–no signal!

Prior to shooting I planned to take readings of grey scale charts on every set and expose after that. In the turmoil of shooting on location and stressed for time I skipped that. Furthermore, it would only have told me the value of mid-grey, not the exposure. When I have Master Gamma on –25 and an electronic viewfinder, that viewfinder is after all the only trustworthy 'light meter'. I was warned about this, but it still shocked me to have to trust a black-and-white viewfinder as you trust your light meter when shooting film. With DigiBeta I, however, never use a light meter anyway, I light by eye and check it with the automatic exposure in the camera from some object close enough to mid-grey.

In order to get maximal use of the viewfinder I kept one zebra reading at 100% signal and the other at 75%. I made sure that there were as few 100% spots in the image as possible, but let there be a lot of 75%, since that is already a very healthy signal. I tried to think of it as exposing a 'fat negative' on film. On people's faces I usually gave tiny bits of 100%, like on the forehead or the eyes, but not on big areas. On our leading ladies' faces (there were some truly beautiful ones) I tried to be even more precise in my exposure. For them I usually gave a tiny bit more 100% on the face than for the men; something similar to what I would have done on film.

I think HD exposure should be treated correctly and with care. Most producers do not understand that HD actually requires more light than 35 mm film. Sometimes you see HD images underexposed, or rather not lit carefully enough, and you end up getting 'ashy' faces, as we call it here. I have noticed that HD turns grey and oddly brown in skin tones if the signal is not healthy. HD productions need the same crew and lighting package as 35 mm film if high-quality standards are to be maintained!

On *Hymypoika* both my lighting time and package were squeezed to a minimum. We tried hard to make the most out of available lights and practicals. Luckily I had the same gaffer as on some of my DigiBeta shoots. He knew roughly what HD required in new situations and locations. We were also often amazed by how deep HD can 'dig' into the shadow areas. Next time I will make sure not to let my lighting package get too small.

Post-production

I had seven days of grading in the Spirit suite at Generator Post in Helsinki. That means exactly 7×8 hours. The final duration of the film is 108 minutes. My colourist was Adam Vandor, one of the three at Generator and my personal choice since we had done many music videos together before. He is very active in the process and gives many creative suggestions, most of them highly beneficial to the final result.

Based on my experiences from my latest film *Elina* (shot on Super 16), I knew that five days would not be enough. I therefore asked for seven days, and got it. We could have managed it in six, but the last day was spent on seeing our grading work with 'fresh eyes' and that was definitely the right thing to do. The director attended the first two days and watched the final

Fig 3.9   DoP Jarkko T. Laine with an HD camera shooting *Hymypoika* (photo: Seppo Louhi)

grading when it was time to lock it. Adam and I found this freedom and confidence inspiring and we felt the same trust for our vision from the producer's side. And we are all very happy with the final result!

Rough Guidelines for Hymypoika Grading

- The look should go hand in hand with the documentary-like approach we had during shooting (all on location, hand-held, two-camera, zoom lenses only, improvised acting, plenty of unlit night exteriors etc.).
- It should not, however, be *too* realistic. It should catch the eye of a young audience, used to consume music videos and commercials in large quantities. Definitely not 'kitchen sink' realistic.
- Helsinki should not look too much like Helsinki (in April not the most glorious place on earth).
- Make the best out of scenes shot in available and uncorrected light. Extend the dirty, green look of metro station fluorescent light and the few neon lights in town to their limits.
- Have a strong touch of *cyan* go through the whole film. Cyan was something I already had in mind while planning the film.

- Keep shadow sides a bit *green,* especially in day exteriors.
- Try to achieve a combination of *orange and green* as a colour guideline for the film.
- Leave blacks very deep, although signal wise leaving them a tiny bit above zero since shoot-out on Kodak Premiere print stock would certainly push them back.
- Try to manage burnt-out highlights as well as we could. We managed them quite well by introducing various white-clipping techniques in grading.

I soon realized that a few of the scenes just hadn't got enough exposure. We managed to save them in grading, but I should have filled shadow areas more on those shots. One nice thing about HD is that blacks remain black. You cannot open those deep shadows later in grading, but at least you can keep them very black.

One of our leading ladies had extremely black hair, and there was obviously no way I could fill-light her hair separately. In many of her scenes I felt that we had to 'sacrifice' quality with blacks getting just too deep. I claim that Super 16 (Vision 500T) would have given much more shadow detail. The latitude of higher speed film stocks is far wider than HD, and, of course, much closer to the way the human eye reads and understands darkness and highlights. I still feel that there is a much wider range of possibilities in terms of digital grading if it is based on film negative than on HD.

I did not face any major grading problems because of our two-camera method. They matched together rather well and intercutting worked. One B-camera shot however, failed because it did not match A-camera exposure in a metro station scene because it was accidentally set at one stop under. It had to be changed to look like low-resolution 'surveillance camera', and it worked. Additional Sony MicroMV-material in the film was also given a rougher look with some horizontal lining in order to look like it had been shot from a video screen or monitor. We wanted to separate this material as far as possible from the HD look, since we wanted HD to look like it was shot on film.

Release Printing

The printing was done on Kodak Premiere stock. Our tests showed that Premiere was far more faithful to the HD master look than Vision. Release prints were made in 1:2.35 ratio, as framed in the cameras (Vista 2). As suggested from our distributor the release prints were made in Technicolor, Rome. Our number of release prints was quite high in Finnish terms, 42 copies, and we got a very good offer from Rome. We tested on two reels and arrived at guiding print light numbers 24-34-17, which seemed to us the closest possible to the look of the HD master. I then spent two days in Rome and already the second answer print was satisfying.

Printmaking did not differ at all from a project originated on film negative. My discussions with my contact person in Rome, Angelo Lofari (custom service manager), taught me that we could have made our HD master even more colourful in grading. That's because the printing tends to 'wash out' colours a little bit. Precise colour reproduction from HD masters to film print is difficult to achieve. Next time I will leave my HD master somewhat more colourful.

A few weeks after grading for cinema we went back to Generator Post to make TV and DVD mastering. This was a session of some 6 hours, going through the film, adding colour here and there, taking off peak colours occasionally, increasing contrast, desaturating selected skin tones etc. No big changes were necessary and I am really happy and proud over how well *Hymypoika* will look on DVD and TV.

Conclusion

In post-production I needed to put all my trust in the staff at Generator Post since this was my first HD picture. Their post-production line for HD video has reached very high international standards. I was at times negative and grumbling during the shoot, faced as I was for the first time with all the drawbacks of HD production. I thank the producers, Riina Hyytiä, Aleksi Bardy and Olli Haikka, for putting up with it and I do look forward to my next HD shoot (haven't I said 'next time I will …' many times in this text?). And by that time many of the technical and practical problems described here will probably be solved. I also sincerely hope that my contribution to this book will be helpful to other first-time HD DoPs.

4

Audio Recording for HD

Simon Bishop

When I first thought about recording audio for HD video cameras, I wondered how or why it should be different in any way from recording audio for film or standard definition. Three years and a number of projects later, I realize that though subtle, the differences are definitely there, and are very real.

Three things that I have found to be most crucial when considering a HD project are:

1   Unwanted on-set noises.
2   What to record on and where.
3   Post-production workflows for audio (and pictures) from shooting to delivery format.

Unwanted On-set Noises

On-set noises have caused problems for sound recordists for years, but digital brings new ones to deal with. Most, if not all HD camcorders, and many HD cameras, are fitted with fans to cool the internal electronics – some have more than one fan. These fans are high-pitched and quite loud, and switch on and off as the camera requires more or less cooling. In the case of camcorders, these fans seem to switch on and off irrespective of whether the machine is recording or not, so it is quite possible that the fans will switch on in the middle of a take. A colleague who recently recorded an HD feature film, told me that on his project they largely got away with these noises because the project had a lot of loudly spoken and leary characters, 'subtle' acting was not a requirement. He also told me, however, that had he been required to record a period piece on HD, then he would have been concerned as to the viability of achieving any usable dialogue when shooting in smaller, intimate, interior locations.

A simple solution would be to let the camera's cooling fan run all the time except when the camera is recording, and thus stop the unwanted noise during that recording time. It is unlikely that the camera would be recording for so long that the internals would overheat, and there could be steps put in place to ensure that the camera will come to no harm, whilst least affecting the sound recording. Not only do the fans in the cameras annoy, but the scanner (rotating head drum) can cause similar unwelcome noises as well. A solution to both of the above could be to use a thick padded leather camera cover (known in film circles as a Barney or blimp). Though these undoubtedly reduce the camera noise to a far more acceptable level, they often block the airflow around the camera body causing the camera to run even hotter and need even more fanning! There are stories of HD cameras overheating in such conditions.

Another source of undesirable on-set noise is the 'video village', as it is often referred to. The video village is the area where one or more, generally large, HD monitors or plasma screens are set up for tech checks and similar. It is usually in this area that technical video 'stuff' gets done – master sync and timecode generation, master (if no camcorder) and/or back-up HD video recording, down conversion to standard definition video for instant on-set playback (which generally involves delaying audio to match the down converted pictures), frame grabs for later matching of shot sizes or lighting for SFX etc.

A whole host of essential processes might be done in the video village, but there is the inevitable catch that, yet again, most of the equipment used in this place relies on internal fanning to keep it cool. The average video village is not a quiet place, so the best thing you can do is to move it as far away (acoustically) from the shooting area as possible. This involves an amount of decision making as to whether you move the village further away from the shooting area to enable sensible sound recording, or keep it closer for communication and practicalities of cable runs etc. A goodly number of people will gather around the monitors at the video village. These people are all human (generally) and invariably the more people that gather, the more shuffling, coughing and other acoustic noises will be made – another good reason for moving the village a little further away from the set.

If you are shooting at a 'real' location – a house or similar – then it is often possible (essential?) to build the village on a different floor of the building, or in a room far enough away for the noise not to be a nuisance. Exterior set-ups are generally less of a problem as there is usually enough urban ambient noise to cover that of the village. A common problem is when you are shooting in a studio with a number of adjacent sets built within one sound stage, and the obvious thing to do is to find somewhere fairly central to build the video village, to ease cable runs and communications etc. This is possibly the worst thing to do for the sound department – the noise of a central video village can often be heard on all of the adjacent sets. Possible solutions might be to use a nearby room for the village, or a Portacabin or a similar demountable structure in a corner of the studio – anything really that might create a solid barrier to stop the unwanted technical noises finding their way to the set. Note that the dedicated recorder recommended for use with the Thomson Viper system is called The Director's Friend. When I attended a demo I counted four large fans whirring away in the back of it – Director's Friend perhaps, but no friend of the sound department for sure!

It is most often the case that the DoP on a HD shoot will want or need an HD monitor close to the camera or set such that he or she might be able to check the lighting and exposure. The larger the monitor then generally the more or larger and/or louder the fans it will contain. It might be wise to give some thought to ways of reducing the noises made by these monitors (polystyrene box built around the back or similar).

There is another source of on-set noise which is peculiar to 24p shoots and is caused by any HMI lighting that may be in use. Most modern HMI ballasts allow the lights to be run in one of two different modes – flicker free and silent, where flicker free is rather noisier (high pitched buzzes and squeals at anywhere from about 6 kHz upwards). Because of the frame rate of a 24p camera, most often HMI lights can only be used in the noisier flicker free mode so may well add to the sound recordist's worries.

What to Record On and Where?

It might seem like an obvious question, but the answers are many and diverse at present. An obvious factor that might affect the sound recordist is where (in terms of media) the pictures are being recorded. If the master pictures are being recorded on a camcorder then it must be decided as to whether master sound is also recorded on that camcorder, or on a separate audio recorder. It might appear to be simplest and most economical to send the sound from the mixer to be recorded on the camcorder, but there are numerous reasons why this might not be a wise practice. One of the most worrying is electrical interference. Video and film sets are far from ideal environments for sending analogue audio signals from one place to another. It can be quite tricky at times to find a route from mixer to recorder where the cables might avoid any forms of electrical interference like HMI head leads, dimmed tungsten lamp cables or similar. It is quite possible that a cable laid earlier along an apparently good route may well be compromised later on by the proximity of some kind of 'naughty' cable, laid unbeknown to the recordist. Moreover, any confidence return from recorder to mixer is likely to involve another cable, which may well take either the same or a different route to the sends and may pick up its own interference. A recordist hearing a buzz or hum on an audio confidence return will have no way of knowing whether the interference is on the send to the camera, or the return from it, or both, and will thus be unable to say instantly whether the recorded sound is acceptable or not. A solution to this dilemma is to record the master audio at the sound recordist's station, where it can be checked locally for any unwanted noises.

If the master audio is to be recorded on a separate recorder at the sound recordist's station, then a few questions occur. These include what audio (if any) you might record simultaneously on to the camcorder, and how it might get there. It would seem wise to get some audio recorded on the camcorder at the time of shooting. This could be as simple as a rough guide track to enable sync checks later on in post-production (could be as basic as camera mic on auto gain, or maybe a fairly good mix sent by radio to the camera). Another method could be to send two (or even four) channels of mixed production audio by cable to the camera. The important thing to remember is that the master sound is being recorded elsewhere, so if there is some kind of a problem getting clean sound to the camcorder it really can be sorted out in post!

If the master audio is recorded anywhere other than on the picture recording device then thought must be given as to how this master audio will be remarried with the pictures (in sync) and at what stage this might happen in the post-production process. Inevitably this will involve timecode of some description. There are various different methods in use at present, and one of the most important decisions to be made before shooting starts is where or what is to be the timecode master clock. It should be remembered that if timecode is to be sent from one machine to another, and the remote machine is to record this incoming timecode, then the remote machine is almost definitely going to need an external sync reference as well as timecode. If using this method then it is usually easiest and most reliable to make a central sync reference and timecode master generation point. Timecode and video syncs can be sent from here to any remote machines that may require them. When using this method it often makes sense to do this at the video village. It is then possible to send syncs (Tri level to cameras, regular to audio recorders or standard definition recorders) and timecode to all the recording devices. This usually involves a lot of cabling, and it should be borne in mind that a fault on any one of these cables could be pretty catastrophic in post-production. Be aware that on-board camera timecode generators are notoriously unreliable, and Sony cameras in particular have been known to lose or gain frames during tape or battery changes.

A more user- (i.e. shooting) friendly method of timecode distribution is to use portable timecode generators, one for each recording device in use, all jammed from a master generator or source. The generators will also need to produce sync pulses, and in the case of HD cameras these should be Tri level syncs in the appropriate format. Ambient of Germany and Denecke in the United States make these generators and they are a good, accurate, reliable, proven and cable-free solution to the timecode issue.

In the latter months of 2003 the choice of what machine to record on has at least doubled, and more choices are due to follow shortly. Quarter-inch tape is pretty much a distant memory, and portable TC DAT recorders are no longer being manufactured. The new technology in audio recording is File Recorders. File-based recorders are hardly new to the business – the Zaxcom Deva II recorder has been in ever-more common use for the past four years, followed more recently by the Nagra V, Fostex PD6, the Aaton Cantar X and the HHB Portadrive. More new multitrack recorders are due during 2004. Fostex, Sound Devices, Zaxcom and possibly others are proposing two channel file recorders, whilst multitrack machines in the late stages of manufacture include Zaxcom Devas 3, 4 and 5. The sound recordist is spoilt for choice for a location recorder at present, after so many years of having a choice of one analogue (Nagra), or two digital (HHB Portadat or Fostex PD-2 or 4) recorders.

High definition pictures become computer files once uploaded into a non-linear edit system, so it makes perfect sense for the audio to be treated in a similar way. Audio recorded as files can be uploaded into NLE systems much faster than real time, and so considerable cost savings can be made in post-production. The new file-based recorders offer a myriad of different track counts and file formats, up to 10 tracks, 24 bit, 192 kHz sampling rate, in any one of at least four file formats, so there is the potential for a lot of data to be recorded in a single day. The files will need to be downloaded to some form of deliverable, most likely at the end of each shooting day, so thought must be given to data rates and transfer times (75 minutes worth of 24 bit, 96 kHz, 10 channel audio would use nearly 13 Gigs of data storage). The hot new delivery format is recordable DVD disc, which is currently supported by the Zaxcom Deva 4 and 5, and the Aaton Cantar recorders.

Post-production Workflows for Audio (and Pictures)

They are essential aids in using these new systems and technologies, both artistically and financially. There are many new software products available for post-production that allow recorded audio files to be used in more efficient ways and ease the post-production process. High-speed batch import of audio files and auto conforming is now a reality, but only works if the workflow is considered and thought out in advance. Now more than ever it is essential that a post-production workflow is designed in advance of any shooting, to ensure that there are no conflicts of file types or formats further down the line. If embarking on an HD project with file-based sound recording, one would be well advised to appoint a post-production supervisor who is well versed in these new technologies, as well as a techno-friendly editor (or at the very least assistant editor) to ensure that the workflows are tested and adhered to during all stages of the production and post-production process.

Figure 4.1 shows a typical audio workflow for multitrack shooting. In this example we are using a product called MetaFlow, which can link the multiple files recorded on a particular take. This enables the editor to cut using just one or two tracks (a 'mixed' track), yet still enables the dialogue editor to track lay using all of the original files recorded (the multiple tracks).

Most if not all of the new file-based recorders allow for input of metadata (think of it as a way of 'bar coding' each recording), which will undoubtedly become of greater significance to post-production in the very near future. Metadata allows us to 'tag' every part of an audio file such that it can be easily found and utilized later on in the process. Software tools now allow us to use metadata to instantly find alternative takes from the same scene or slate number, and new applications for metadata appear with great regularity. Metadata is one of the new buzzwords in post-production, but is also relevant to original production audio. A well-designed workflow will include instructions as to how metadata should be applied to the original location recordings, such that they can be easily used throughout the

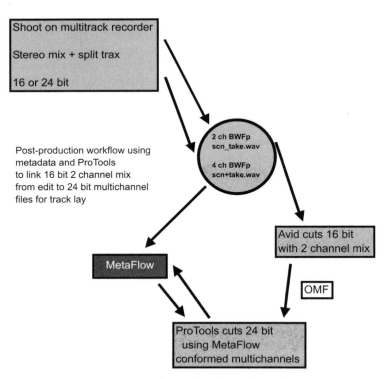

Fig 4.1   Audio workflow for multitrack shooting using MetaFlow.

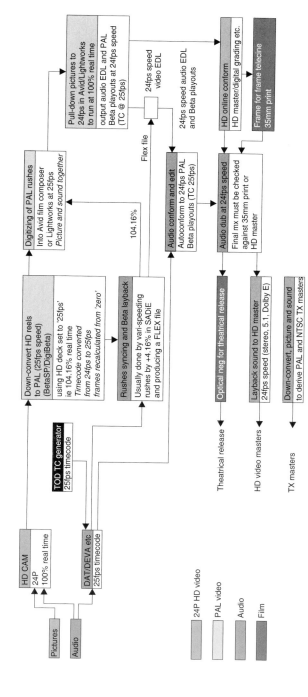

Fig 4.2   24p/PAL post-production route 1: syncing up sound to PAL rushes by vari-speeding in SADiE (courtesy Dave Turner, Videosonics).

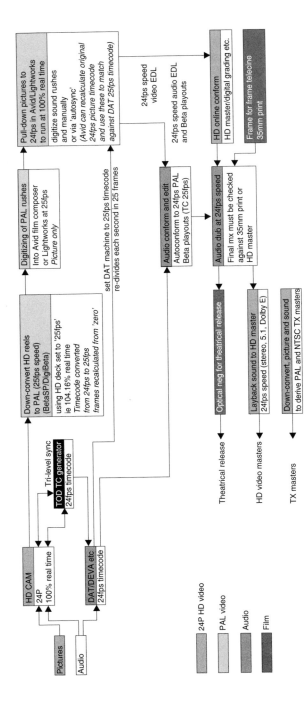

Fig 4.3 24p/PAL post-production route 2: syncing up sound in Avid/Lightworks (courtesy Dave Turner, Videosonics).

post-production process. This is still an emerging technology, but is in use now, so care should be taken to get it right all the way through the workflow. Designing an efficient workflow will reap time and cost savings in post-production, and allow more time for creative decisions to be made, and thus improve soundtracks.

Figures 4.2 and 4.3 show 24p PAL post-production routes. These two different workflows could be used for post-producing a 24p HD shoot. Method 1 accommodates the Avid quirk, where most Avids cannot run at 24fps. This method involves syncing up on a DAW (SADiE) or similar by vari-speeding the audio to 104.16% such that the audio matches the 24–25 frame converted pictures. Method 2 keeps most of the post-production at 24 fps and involves syncing up in the Avid. (My thanks to Dave Turner of Videosonics for permission to use his workflow diagrams.)

5
Introduction to the Digital Intermediate Process

Steve Shaw

Digital Intermediate vs. Digital Film

The term 'digital intermediate' describes a process that is nominally one-third of the operation loosely termed digital film. The other two-thirds encompass acquisition (the obtaining of the source material through some form of capture) and presentation (the distribution, projection and/or transmission of the final result, also known as D-cinema or E-cinema, although these terms are also used to mean the whole digital film chain – see Chapter 1 for definitions).

A major point about these three processes is that they are all independent of one another, and inclusion of one process in a project does not immediately require the involvement of the other two. Therefore digitally acquired material can just as easily be projected via traditional celluloid means as via a digital projector and equally as likely film originated material may be shown digitally via a digital projector (see Fig. 5.2). The digital intermediate (DI) process is therefore applicable for traditional film projects (acquired and presented) as well as those classified as 'digital', through the use of digital capture or projection techniques. The DI process is chosen on the benefits it provides for the project in question, not the use of any additional digital technology elsewhere within the project.

Fig 5.1 Intermediate process independent of I/O.

Benefits of the DI Process

The DI process, in its most basic form, can be considered as a replacement for the opto/chemical film lab environment offering digital neg cutting from

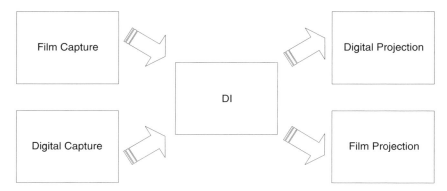

Fig 5.2   The independence of film and digital processes.

offline edit information, optical transition processes such as wipes and dissolves and film grading aimed at producing the equivalent of a timed IP (interpositive), although the resultant output from a DI lab will inevitably be a timed negative.

This base level of operation is the heart of a DI lab and through its ability to provide enhancements throughout the process can be a strong reason for it to be chosen in preference to the traditional chemical lab.

The benefits it offers range from almost unlimited flexibility, with multiple variations available for assessment immediately, without need to process and project film, to a guarantee of quality regardless of the number or complexity of optical processes undergone. To be able to sit within a DI environment and see, interactively, changes as they are made is a film producer's/director's/DoP's dream. To be able to try a dissolve between two scenes, followed by an alternate wipe to assess the difference is an impossibility outside of the DI environment for film projects.

In general, the things we have taken for granted for years within the longform video market have been all but impossible for film-based projects. And have you ever attempted to sit and work at a traditional film grading or timing station? The operator's screen is about 6 inches wide and often of indeterminate playback speed! Compare that to grading via a 32 inch HD film colorimetry monitor or digital projector on a full size theatre screen with real time 2K playback!

Beyond such basic benefits the DI environment offers advanced capabilities that have previously been held within the domain of the VFX film. For some considerable time film effects work has been carried out almost exclusively by digital techniques. However, the only films that have gained access to such tools have been comparatively high budget projects, produced with digital VFX written into the storyline. With the DI environment projects that would traditionally have never budgeted for digital are now able to take advantage of the benefits it offers, without having to find ways to increase the project budget.

To enable this has taken a major change in the underlying digital technology to enable a digital workflow akin to that found within traditional labs, effectively moving away from the previous distributed workflow environment of digital VFX to a more integrated (hero) environment enjoyed within chemical labs and video longform post houses.

In simplified form, a DI environment needs to be a centralized and self-contained environment enabling all necessary DI functions to be carried out without the need to move operations. This is explained further later in this chapter but suffice to say if you are moving data between environments, allowing for the need to relocate complex VFX shots, you are losing time and money.

Operating Parameters of the DI Process

Having introduced the concept of DI, the process itself requires more understanding. It is not enough to simply describe it as a 'digital lab'. What are the parameters within which the digital lab must be able to operate if it is to function acceptably? What steps must be taken to get material into and out of the lab? How can the entire process be calibrated? And what toolset is required to perform the necessary DI functions?

If we accept that the DI process aims to digitally master a film in its entire form there are a number of parameters any DI system must be able to meet, assuming major compromise is not acceptable.

- Provide controlled input to output calibration, including working with different colour space, bit depth, resolution and format images.
- Hold an entire film, with handles and variants, in full film resolution (whatever that is?).
- Auto conform from an offline EDL with ability to compare online to offline for verification.
- Playback the entire film project in real time, with temps/animatics/previews as necessary, at full resolution.
- Display the film images in true 'film' colorimetry, contrast, gamma, etc.
- Respond immediately to changes for review and sign-off.
- Perform the basic functions necessary for a DI operation to proceed, including editing, opticals, colour correction, VFX work, titles, etc.
- Work with accepted technical image parameters to present a final image quality acceptable as 'film' (?).

As is to be expected, such a list of requirements raises more questions than it answers, with 'what exactly is digital film?' being uppermost amongst them.

What follows is a discussion on the main point of interest, evaluating possible options and approaches, including technical reasoning as well as realistic business requirements. Two of the first questions people raise when discussing digital film are what resolution and what bit depth? The questions have two very different answers.

Bit Depth

To take the easiest first. Original camera negative, depending on film stock, has a dynamic range capable of recording detail both well into shadow (blacks) as well as into highlights (whites). Such dynamic range enables decisions on contrast, brightness and colour balance, in RGB (CMY) to be made during the post-production (film lab) process, ensuring the DoP's views are seen in the final film. It is the print film stock that extracts from the wide dynamic range camera negative a realistic dynamic range suitable for human viewing.

This process, from negative to print, occurs because at no point during the shooting process can anyone be sure what exposure detail the film is actually recording. By having a wide dynamic range negative any errors can therefore be corrected in the lab.

As much DI work will originate from film camera negative it makes sense that the DI process offers a similar level of dynamic range. This can be through the use of 10 bit log data or 13 bit (or greater) lin data to maintain the full dynamic range with a good level of granularity (brightness change per sample), although 10 bit lin may be acceptable in some circumstances due to the WhatYouSeeIsWhatYouGet (WYSIWYG) nature of the digital DI process. The final decision depends on the approach being taken to the DI process and at what point a 'timed digital internegative/positive' is being produced. For flexibility and security this is usually the final stage (colour correction being performed after all editing and VFX work has been completed), requiring a wide dynamic range of material.

There are relatively few disagreements on this, allowing for pragmatism and business requirements to shape the needs.

A Note on Log vs. Lin

There is a lot of confusion regarding the use of log or lin data. In truth the question should be what is the dynamic range that is best to use and then what is the best method to digitally hold the range of that image.

As has been discussed already, original camera negative film has very wide latitude, which is another way to say it has the ability to simultaneously see detail deep into shadows and high into bright areas of an image. To experience what this means stand facing a window opening out on to a bright day. If you look out the window you will be unable to see (via your peripheral vision) detail surrounding the bright window – everything will appear dark and detail-less. If you chose to look away from the window (to one side) you will now be able to see detail within the room but outside the window will now appear blown-out, without any detail. This is because the combination of deep shadow and bright sunlight is beyond the ability of the human eye to capture. The eye's dynamic range is too small. Original camera negative film, on the other hand, can see both simultaneously.

Film also sees (records) illumination (brightness) as logarithmic information, which is also true of the human eye. That is to say that within shadow detail a small change in illumination is easily seen but that the same level of change in bright areas hardly registers. Imagine being in a dark room and someone across the other side strikes a match. It will be immediately apparent. However, if the room is now filled with sunlight and a match is struck again, it will be all but invisible.

The problem is that the devices used to turn image data into digital information (CCDs – charge coupled devices) output an analogue voltage signal that is a linear response to the illumination they see. This is then converted into a digital signal that represents the linear analogue signal – linear digital data.

As small changes in shadow detail are easy to see the illumination change per digital sample needs to be very small, but as the digital conversion is linear this means that the same number of samples per illumination change will be used in highlight areas too – with the result that many samples in the highlight areas will be redundant as the perceived changes in brightness will be too small for the human eye to see.

If the dynamic range being digitized is not large this is not too much of a problem, which is what happens with digital cameras when 4 to 5 stops of illumination information is captured. With 10 bit data providing 1023 samples there are enough to represent shadow detail accurately and not too many wasted in highlight areas.

If the dynamic range is the same as original camera negative film – 10 to 11 stops – it will take 13 bit linear data providing a staggering 8192 samples to match the granularity of each sample in the shadow detail to that of the lower dynamic range image, with a lot of redundant samples in the highlights. This makes the data file huge in comparison to the 10 bit linear file.

However, if the large dynamic range information is converted into digital log data only the necessary samples will be maintained, with plenty in the shadows and highlights. In this way 10 bit log data can faithfully represent the full 11 stops of illumination information!

This is the basis for the Kodak specified CIN digital film file format where each digital sample represents 0.002 density of a camera original negative, which is below the threshold of human sight perception (i.e. you never see digital 'banding' or steps between sample value – LSB – 'least significant bit' changes).

In this way log information can be viewed as a form of loss-less compression and is the ideal data format for digital film DI work.

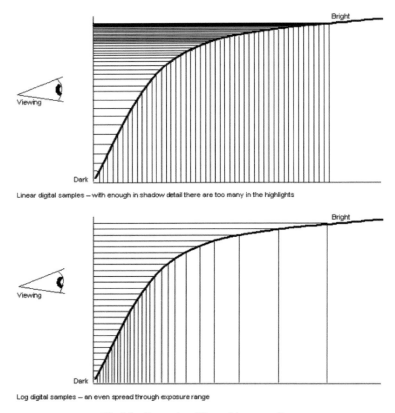

Fig 5.3 Example of lin and log sampling.

Linear Data in a Log World?

Additionally, the ability of log data to hold extended brightness range information from the start can be used as a benefit when working with image data captured via a linear source such as an HD camera.

This is difficult to explain, so bear with me ...

Linear capture devices such as most HD cameras, all SD cameras and telecines when not set to log mode capture the scene/image they are looking at by setting artificial black and white points. Any detail below or above these points is clipped. However, with careful control this clipping can be minimized on all but the widest dynamic range scenes/images. But, all the available data samples are now used up in holding the initial image so if any grading is performed within iQ in the same linear space additional clipping will occur as the image is pushed higher or lower.

However, if the initial linear data is mapped into log space the initial linear black 0 (zero)–actually 65 but with no valid data below 65 – point gets set to 95 and the initial white 1023 (actually 940 but with no valid data above) to 685, providing huge additional head and foot room for grading. Remember that you have also moved from a linear colour space to log colour space so the new granularity of sample (brightness change per digital sample) has effectively improved throughout the range too. The result is much better graded images.

Even if not going back to film, the use of print D-log E-style log to lin conversion Luts at the output stage to the VTR can maintain more of the new head room than normal simple log to lin conversions where 95 is again clipped to black and 685 to white.

Note: although the above description discusses log vs. lin, in truth what is called linear is in reality TV gamma data which has a non-linear response in an attempt to go some way to dealing with the issues mentioned here for pure linear data – part way between lin and log if you like. White is also set

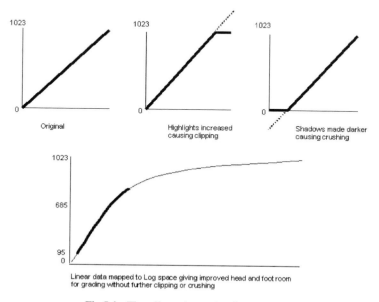

Fig 5.4 The effect of mapping linear data to log space.

to 940 and black to 65 allowing some head room but that cannot be seen in a standard viewing environment – i.e. at home – as any values from 0 to 65 and 940 to 1023 are illegal and are clipped. This is not true of 'data' systems where all levels are valid. However, to go into this in depth will confuse the issue. If you are interested you can research further at your leisure.

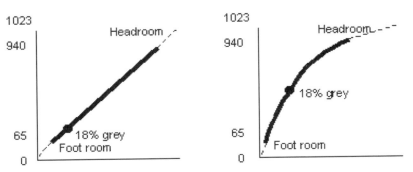

Fig 5.5   Linear vs. TV Gamma

Resolution

To turn now to the second question – resolution. This is slightly different. All cameras are WYSIWYG with regard to image framing. Therefore it is very unlikely that a scene will be shot 'wider' than required to allow for a zoom in post-production (variations in full-frame, Academy, 1:85, etc. accepted). However, as with dynamic range, the traditional chemical film process of generating a final print for viewing does change the resolution of the material from that held on the original camera negative. Therefore, although the original negative may have a resolution near equal to 4K digital pixels (3K is actually more accurate – even though some people talk of 6K) the reality is that such numbers don't allow for optical losses via camera lenses, discussing only the 'perfect' capture ability of fine grain negative stock – not a real-world situation. Due to these losses, and further losses throughout the film processing operation, the final projection print has a resolution more closely represented by 1K pixels. This obviously depends on the number of intermediate stages undergone and the quality of the processes used, but represents a true situation for the average release print film.

To bring a little bit of true life into this, while grading *Pinocchio* for digital projection and working at 1280 × 1024 resolution, the director and main actor, Roberto Benigni, was surprised to find his 'frown lines' visible in the digital projected final when they were not in the film print. As a result we had to 'soften' the focus (blur it!) on the digital final – and I won't tell you how we did this but is wasn't via digital technology!

Therefore, what is the correct resolution for the DI process? 3K or even 4K may be a true representation of the negative, and therefore desirable for long term archive of material that may require future work, such as restoration, but is easily overkill for DI operations based on the generation of a final result for immediate distribution from a clean, new negative that can be held for future generations if necessary. There are serious doubts on the need for this, as the goal for any film project is the deliverable, not the source material, and all restoration processes aim to restore a deliverable – no one will pay to see a negative! And remember, the original 'view' of the director, DoP, etc. has little to do with the negative and everything to do with the final print where he or she can recreate what they 'saw' while shooting, which often has little to do with what is actually on the negative.

As the DI process does away with much of the need to perform multiple intermediates its output can be considered qualitatively superior and capable of maintaining resolution through processes that cause losses through the traditional chemical lab. Therefore, scanning the original negative for a 2K DI process will result in a final image of superior quality to the chemical process equivalent, making 2K, or even less, more than acceptable for the DI process, especially if nyquist over-sampling is used to generate the 2K data for the DI process from a higher resolution scan.

Note: For VFX work being intercut with original camera negative (i.e. not going through a DI process) 2K is the realistic minimum as the digitally generated output negative will go through the same dupe processes as the original negative.

Scientifically, the above approach can be verified through empiric testing. The MTF (Modulation Transfer Function) of any given process can be measured and qualitative comparisons made showing the various losses through lenses, contact printing, aerial printing, film stocks used, etc. This has been performed a number of times by industry bodies and manufacturing companies alike, and the results are available for all to see. As an example, in 2001 the ITU undertook a study that concluded that perfectly exposed and processed 35 mm film when projected in a good cinema has a resolution of just 600–750 lines.

For an understandable approach to film and its characteristics look at the latest Quantel Digital Fact Book.

Less scientific, but equally important, the number of films originated on digital formats of less than 2K resolution (George Lucas' *Star Wars: Episodes I and II* – the prequels – being an obvious example, shot in HD at 1920 pixels by 1080 lines) shows what is truly possible. We can all point to specific scenes where things don't look right, regardless of the film and capture format used. Quality owes a lot more to technique than technology in the majority of cases!

So we now have a system that is defined technically as 2K resolution (2048 × 556/1536 for full aperture 35 mm film) and 10 bit log (or 13 bit lin!) bit depth. Such a system will produce a result suitable for final film output for celluloid projection or for digital mastering for digital projection. The same data can also be used to generate all additional deliverables, such as video, TV, DVD, etc., making the process even more effective.

Greater than 2K?

Although we have shown 2K to be the ideal resolution for DI work, that does not preclude the use of higher resolutions where applicable. For example, when using large matte painting background plates for pan and scan within a 2K window. Also, the use of 4K scanning to produce 2K images via nyquist sampling will maintain resolution far better than a native 2K scan. This is because physically scanning at the same resolution as the theoretical maximum of the source material is not guaranteed to maintain the full resolution or detail of the original.

Consider this. You have 2048 alternate black and white lines recorded onto an Academy OCN film frame. This is probably the maximum resolving power of the film showing its maximum line pairs per millimetre. If you now scan this with a 2048 pixel CCD one of two things is likely to happen (OK – one of a varied number of results but the two extremes will show the theory).

If the CCD cells happen to align exactly with each black and white line the digital result will be perfect as shown in Fig. 5.6. However, if the CCD cells are half a line out they will see half a black line and half a white line at the same time, with the result that the CCD will see near grey (Fig. 5.7)!

While this is an excessive example, it does show how detail can be lost even if scanning (sampling) at the same maximum resolution of the source image.

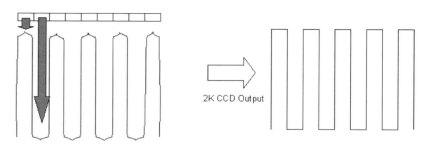

Fig 5.6   Aligned 2K CCD sampling of 2K resolution.

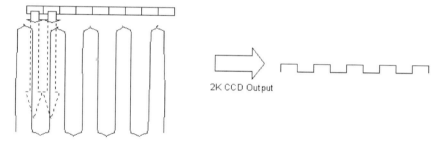

Fig 5.7   Offset 2K CCD sampling of 2K resolution.

If we now double the number of CCD cells to 4096 we are always going to see the underlying image detail and can then nyquist sample down to the original 2K resolution while maintaining almost all of the frequency detail.

Figure 5.8 shows a near perfect alignment but from it the reader can extrapolate what would be seen if the CCD cells were aligned differently – there would always be an output from the CCD that showed a good representation of the waveform from which a high quality 2K image can be generated.

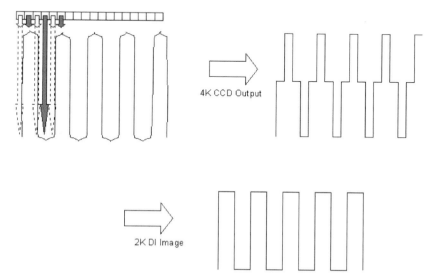

Fig 5.8   Offset 4K CCD sampling of 2K resolution with Nyquist to 2K data.

It is worth saying though that most scanning devices used CCD cells (or flying spots!) that are not directly equal to the image area they are sampling, resulting in better detail representation than one might expect. This tends to make the argument for nyquist sampling less of an issue than it may at first appear. Its always best to perform empirical testing for yourself and define your best methodology.

Equally important from a business perspective, a 2K image requires about 12 Mb of data per 10 bit log RGB frame. A 4K image requires about 48 Mb of data, a 1K image 3 Mb and a video SD image 1 Mb. This shows the level of technology investment required to manipulate 4K vs. 2K vs. 1K, which has a direct impact on the cost of film production and therefore the profitability of any given film project based on the number of 'bums' paying to sit on seats to see the film. Joe Public is unlikely to be willing to pay more to see a 4K processed film versus an HD film, except for an occasional IMAX-style outing!

6

The Economics of Digital Cinema–the Benefits of Change

Sean Foley

A digital cinema production is more cost-effective than a traditional film production. The full scale adoption and standardization of digital cinema technology by the motion picture industry will signify a fundamental change in the way movies are made and exhibited. It is my hope that digital acquisition and computer software will bring the cost of filmmaking lower than ever, eventually relieving the art of filmmaking of Hollywood's damaging tendency, its hegemony. At the end of *Heart of Darkness: A Filmmaker's Apocalypse*, the 1991 documentary about the making of *Apocalypse Now!*, Francis Ford Coppola delivers an almost melancholy prophecy: 'To me, the great hope is that now these little 8 mm video recorders are around and people who normally wouldn't make movies are going to be making them. And suddenly, one day some little girl from Ohio is going to be the new Mozart and make a beautiful film with her father's camcorder … the so-called professionalism about movies will be destroyed forever and it will really become an art form.'

Today filmmaking is on the verge of becoming entirely transparent. One may shoot, post-produce and exhibit all with the same material and the same type of equipment. The little girl with the camcorder can edit her film with her brother's computer and will soon be able to upload her final cut to any digital theatre around the world.

Economic Implications

Let me try to explain and analyse the short term implications of digital cinema and also imagine the eventual effect an entirely digital process will have on the economy of filmmaking and film distribution. What I will describe is a technology that is poised to become the standard for motion picture process and the business that is growing out of this technology.

After all, technology does indeed drive business. The movie created the movie industry.

Today, making content digitally is cheaper than dealing with film. Filmmakers can acquire content digitally at a resolution sometimes equivalent to that of many 35 mm camera negatives. Exhibitors can project this content in theatres at its native resolution, at least two to three times the resolution of an average 35 mm release print. Filmmakers may now record sound and picture onto the same media simultaneously, eliminating the cost of synchronization. Distributors no longer need to make copies or ship them. Filmmakers can edit any format whatsoever on their PowerBook, one can even control the camera with the same PowerBook. Distributors no longer need to subtitle prints. HD cameras and lenses are now designed for 'cine' environments as well as television environments, making the mechanical process of filmmaking finally available for digital acquisition.

Digital implies greater flexibility and often the opportunity to cut costs at most points in the filmmaking process. Cutting out the lab most of all reduces the cost of distributing films, but it also considerably affects the economy of shooting. An efficient production can anticipate spending 25% less money overall if it employs a digital workflow.

It is difficult to predict the actual cost savings of making a digital feature until the technology is fully adopted, as the prices for stock, equipment rentals and labour will depend on the local infrastructure available to support it. There are indeed many opinions about how much cheaper HD is than film. That is obviously because each project treats the medium differently. There are also many opinions about which technology is best. First, understand that digital cinema is essentially movies without the photochemical process. The result is that acquisition, post-production, distribution and exhibition are finally transparent. This fact transforms the business of filmmaking. Total transparency of the medium implies that filmmakers may one day project live into a movie theatre from anywhere in the world. This is what happened to television. When the industry started to depend on tape as a recording medium, the economy of creating and providing content changed fundamentally.

Currently, HD camera packages, post-production solutions and exhibition systems are expensive because of initial investments and the risks involved in offering these new technologies. Everyone knows that new technologies always cost a lot when they first come to the market. For now there is more demand for conventional film and higher price tags are attached to digital cinema. There are, however, current persuasive economic solutions and artistic intentions that encourage the contemporary artist, producer and distributor to go digital now.

A producer seeking the cheapest production/post-production will find that HD is affordable and available. Open the catalogue of this year's Sundance Film Festival and you will see that at least half of the films presented are shot in HD. Digital video projection is also a major part of the regular festival programme. This year, Sundance exhibited five public digital screening locations and one press location. Today, an independent producer may choose to finish their film in HD and only make a 35 mm negative in the case of distribution. This possibility should encourage producers to produce more HD films and take more risks. The power to make current, relevant, and challenging movies will come from democratizing filmmaking as an independent and individual mode of expression. The alternative is that filmmaking becomes more institutionalized and academic. Producers, distributors and filmmakers must accept that digital technology will provide more people with more ways to make more movies. The market will have to adjust and the academy will eventually have to recognize the shift.

D-Cinema – an Independent Filmmaker's Medium

High definition D-cinema is at this point in history an independent film-maker's medium. Shooting HD can cost 20–40% less than shooting on film. An independent producer who is accustomed to making low budget features for less than a couple of million dollars would be foolish to choose film instead of HD. With HD a producer saves money and also gains extra control of the project. Without the high prices of stock, developing and post-production lab work, a producer can substantially reduce the chance of going over budget and can eventually choose to commit to projects that would have once been considered too risky. For now, savings from not having to do work-print rushes from film to tape are considerably offset by the cost of conforming digital back to film for distribution. Once digital distribution and exhibition are part of the industry infrastructure, these reductions can be directly accounted for. Producers who make movies without the assurance of distribution can already take advantage of HD technology by shooting and exhibiting at festivals in HD. Such a move can save at least 80 000 Euro during shooting and 45 000 Euro in post.

A digital workflow conceivably streamlines a production, saving valuable time. Eliminating the need for a lab saves the costs of developing, printing and syncing. Recording stock decreases by a factor of 30 when compared to Super 16 mm and by 98 when compared to 35 mm. There is no more shipping to and from the lab and less time is spent loading and re-loading the camera.

Shooting digital also eliminates telecine in order to view dailies and edit, cutting the negative in order to print, and creating intermediates for implementing effects. Without being tied down to a lab, a digital production is also more autonomous. A crew can go anywhere in the world and make a movie a lot more easily by choosing a digital workflow: no more umbilical cord with the lab.

With a 25% cost saving, and the possibility for quicker turnaround, the HD format seems ideal. However, this analysis misses some components, including the rental of HD equipment and post-production facilities, which are currently relatively expensive due to availability. It also does not consider the impact of social systems in the production process. Learning curves associated with new equipment and new workflow can slow a crew, while the experience of a film trained crew can save time working with traditional cameras and traditional process, yielding a better creative output.

An independent digital project can still achieve a higher quality with greater ease and at less expense. A film shot and processed with the most advanced digital equipment can be cheaper to produce than an average 35 mm production. Independent filmmakers have a moral obligation to use technology to cut costs and to expand techniques. The transformation of the industry to digital offers many opportunities, especially for business development. It is important for us to influence the industry to proliferate its content and to bring more digital films, more frequently, to theatres. It may well involve a sort of compromise until digital reaches the quality and level of perceptual impact that film has, but embracing change is more important. Some of the industry may site the devastating impact that this change may have on jobs. It may be true that, in the short term, many jobs will be cut; but, just imagine the number of jobs that will be created if the industry accepts the change. More movies will certainly mean more jobs.

Digital Exhibition and Festivals

Digital technology will inevitably change the way films are programmed in theatres. Films that do not get a chance under the 35 mm distribution model may be a lot more easily brought to the big screen. Apparently the screenings at this year's Sundance Film Festival (2004) were so packed that many people were turned away at the door. Festivals offer movies that may only be available to a select public a few times. They may never be distributed and never be seen again. The people that do see these movies are the people that have made the trip to the festival venue and have been lucky or important enough to get a seat. Independent filmmaking ends up being elitist when it need not be. Distributors are not directly at fault for this. They do not pick up more movies, especially risky ones, because the cost of distributing a film in 35 mm is so great. Distributors and the exhibitors are in fact slaves to the studios – and how can you blame them? Business is business, and movies are big business. I believe that once cinema is entirely digital, distributors will become much more influential as they will have more freedom in composing their programmes. Dynamic programming will also be encouraged by the fact that theatres will be in no rush to return prints to distributors; because there will be no more prints. Today there are more movies being made than ever, and that indicates that filmmaking is healthy and alive. Now, the majority of movies never reach the public. Exhibitors have no choice but to evolve and respond to the populist, pluralist and international tendencies of twentyfirst-century cinema. If there is no change, the art of filmmaking will become academic.

Imagine what will happen if Sundance, or any festival for that matter, will be able to simultaneously screen movies all over the world. When digital projection is standard then this will conceivably be possible. The festival could beam content by satellite to any number of participating theatres around the globe. This consequence exposes profound potentials for democracy, and capitalism.

The adoption of digital technology will most of all impact the economy of the motion picture industry at the distribution and exhibition level. Digital content will be beamed to theatres via satellites, or transferred on optical discs or by fibre-optic networks, potentially eliminating the several month lag overseas viewers endure for a big Hollywood production. Subtitles, even advertisements, can be swapped in and out minutes before show time. At the theatre, a digital film is stored on a computer server connected to any number of digital projectors. Each projector is equipped with a computer chip that cleans up the image and is capable of showing 35 trillion colour variations. It only requires one individual to operate an entire multiplex of screens. No more hairs, scratches, pops. Instead you get ear-pleasing digital surround sound and clean, crisp images. You can even drop in and out commercials to generate additional revenue for theatres. As it will be possible to incorporate any medium originating on HD, including sports events and live concerts, movie theatres will expand their functions. There is obviously massive financial potential here. Take only the price of a digital copy versus a 35 mm one: 200 Euro for a digital copy and 3000 Euro for a 35 mm print that eventually wears out.

Screen Digest reports that in the United States, a recent surge in investment by theatre chains and technology companies indicates that the number of digital projectors in cinemas will more than double to over 400 in the next 12 months. The UK Film Council has committed some 13 million pounds to pay for the roll-out of 250 digital screens across Britain by 2005. India has embarked on one of the most ambitious digital cinema investment programmes. This year it will wire up an average of 20 cinemas per month. Substantial new investment is also under way in China and in Sweden.

Achieving the benefits of digital workflow requires process changes. There is a need for role changes as well, as the processes are defined around workers and the technology they use. Given that the transition to digital production is inevitable in the view of industry experts, and that new processes will need to be defined, a question arises of how these new technical systems can be integrated with the social systems already in place. Eastman Kodak just announced a 20% cut back of its global workforce.

This is evidence that the greatest economic effect of digital technology will be internal to the industry. Many more jobs will be cut and new jobs will be created. The industry will continue to make more movies and more money. What will change is the quality and availability of digital technology. It will become a lot easier to make a digital movie, and a lot cheaper to distribute it.

Case Study

I have recently participated in a feature project shot on HDCAM and presented on 35 mm at the Berlin Film Festival. We rented the camera (Sony HDW-F900), lenses and monitors for 700 Euro/day and paid 40 Euro per 42 minute HDCAM cassette (50 tapes total). Our HD material was conformed and colour corrected with a Quantel eQ and subsequently output to 35 mm internegative by way of Arri Laser. After serious negotiation, the internegative, one copy, subtitles and sound optical cost 45 000 Euro. The print is excellent; it is almost comparable to a print made from 35 mm original camera negative.

We also brought with us to Berlin an HDCAM cassette of the film, which the festival organizers enabled us to screen in one of their big rooms. The tape was not corrected for such an exhibition; it was simply a dub of what we had delivered for television. Present were the director, the producers, the editor, the colourist, the production designer and a few other colleagues. One producer, who works for a major television channel and knows little about post-production other than the price tag, told me that she did not see much difference between the HD and the 35 mm print. The experts in the room saw the differences. The blacks were generally less rich, and the image was in a way less lively, less luminescent. I imagine that tweaking the image in post and making some advancements in the technology of digital projection would do the trick. At the same time the image was already at least two times more defined, clearer, and sharper. The average moviegoer does not notice the difference between HD and 35 mm. It is standard knowledge that an HD to 35 mm workflow delivers a higher quality print than a Super 16 to 35 mm blow-up. The next generation of cameras, projectors and lenses will undoubtedly deliver a cinematic image that will rival the current 35 mm standard for acquisition and exhibition. I did no look at our HD test projection as a comparison to our print as much as I looked at it as if I were looking at what the cinematic experience will eventually become. I was blown away to have the projectionist sitting in the audience with me and adjusting the projector with a remote control. Whatever we may love about film, we must say goodbye to it.

This particular feature film cost 500 000 Euro to make. Shooting Super 16 mm would have cost at least 30 000 Euro more, and 35 mm, at least 100 000 Euro more. I would rather buy additional days of shooting then spend such a sum on a '*beaux arts*' aesthetic, which is bound to fade away like the long-playing record, the typewriter, and the handwritten manuscript have.

I am always impressed when I go to a laboratory. All those massive machines and people in white smocks who are dedicated to operating on images. It is mysterious; I love it, and I wish film would be around forever. It is alive, it smells. However, soon labs will be no more, and maybe we will finally get rid of the idea that you need a lot of money to make movies.

7

Some Recent European Initiatives in Digital Film Production, Distribution and Exhibition

7.1   European Digital Cinema Forum (EDCF),
By John Graham

The European Digital Cinema Forum (EDCF) is the pivotal organization for all digital cinema interests in Europe.

Aims

EDCF was formed to enable the creation of a technical and business framework for the harmonious introduction of D- and E-cinema in Europe.

The EDCF represents all elements in the chain from content creators through to exhibition:

- The cinema industry – including producers, distributors, exhibitors.
- The industrials – manufacturers, telcos etc.
- The institutions – including government bodies, film institutes, associations, etc.

Following a number of European conferences and seminars where the cultural and technological risks and opportunities presented by digital projection were recognized, the Forum was formed in 2001 by the CST and CNC in France, the DTI and BKSTS in the UK and the Swedish Film Institute. The importance of creating a unified European voice to talk with the United States on the question of universal, interoperable standards for D-cinema was also a driving force behind the creation of the Forum (see Chapter 9 on Standards).

In addition to enhancing the cinema experience for audiences, digital projection technology, in its various forms, offers the opportunity to provide high-quality cinema in communities that currently do not have access to cinema. It also provides the opportunity to support and develop local European cultures and will provide greater access and opportunities for development in the smaller filmmaking communities in Europe.

The aim of the EDCF is to encourage the flow of information, share experiences and ensure the closest possible cooperation and synergy amongst all interested parties world wide.

The Forum aims to facilitate the introduction of digital cinema in such a way that this will result in more cinema and will guard against dominance by a few large corporations.

Structure

The EDCF, 2003, was managed by a Steering Board compromising:

- Ase Kleveland, SFI, Sweden, President
- Charles Sandbank, DTI, UK, Vice President
- Jean Menu, CNC, France, Vice President
- Matthieu Sintas, CST, France
- Anders Geertsen, DFI, Denmark
- Johannes Lassila, FFPA, Finland
- Kees Ryninks, NFF, Netherlands
- Lasse Svanberg, SFI, Sweden
- Peter Wilson, Snell & Wilcox, UK
- John Graham, BKSTS, UK, Secretariat

The EDCF has three working Modules composed of industry professionals who tackle specific problems in their areas of activity:

- **Content Module** chaired by Johannes Lassila, whose plans for 2004 include the delivery of this present publication and developing a database for alternative digital content.
- **Commercial Module**, chaired by Anders Geertsen, which will be developing business models and collecting and analysing market information.
- **Technical Module**, chaired by Peter Wilson, which is working with colleagues in the United States to establish technical standards for D-cinema.

Establishing Period

During its 18 month formative period, the EDCF has been funded by the CNC, Swedish Film Institute and the DTI (UK). The BKSTS (UK) has provided secretariat services to the Forum.

Constitution and the Future

Membership stands at 256 (February 2004) and is represented in most European Countries. The EDCF has become known and respected throughout the world and is seen to be an essential body in determining the future direction of digital cinema content and technology. There is a particularly strong and constructive dialogue established with Hollywood studios on matters of technical standards and interoperability.

Having achieved this position on a relatively short time scale, the Forum was established formally under Dutch law as a Stichting (Foundation) during the summer of 2003.

Subscriptions for membership were introduced in January 2004. Further information about the work of the EDCF can be found on the website www.edcf.net.

7.2   National Film Theatre Digital Test Bed, *By Sarah Trigg and Richard Boyd*

Why a Digital Test Bed?

The rate at which digital cinema technology is progressing across the globe can be seen as both a blessing and a potential hazard. There are still many issues that need to be resolved before the film industry as a whole can be confident about what the future holds. Agreements have yet to be made on resolution and standardization issues, and although this is being addressed globally, because of the wide and varying differences of opinion between all those associated with film production and exhibition, it will be some time before any conclusions are drawn.

The technology itself is also developing at an alarming rate, and while the UK Film Council has just announced that it will be investing approximately 13 million pounds in 2K projection, the first 4K projector prototype from NTT in Japan has just been demonstrated in the UK. Questions about massive investment now in technology that could be redundant in five years' time need to be addressed and this is one of the reasons for the reluctance of commercial exhibitors to invest in digital technology. While filmmakers strive for the perfect picture, distributors strive for cheaper distribution methods and the manufacturers are vying for attention – the audiences at present do not seem to be concerned one way or the other whether they watch a digital or 35 mm film. Having said that, recent audience responses to the screening of Warner's digitalized classics *Casablanca, Singin' in the Rain* and *The Adventures of Robin Hood* at the National Film Theatre (NFT) have been overwhelmingly positive.

The Digital Test Bed (DTB) at the NFT was born out of the need for an independent and neutral testing facility for exploring the new digital technology that is already having an impact on cinema exhibition and film-making. The inspiration came out of the industry cooperation that resulted in the road-show 'Celluloid or Silicon?', which toured London, Glasgow, Cardiff, Bradford and Belfast in November to December 2000 and was funded by the DTI (Department of Trade and Industry) and DCMS (Department for Culture, Media and Sport). There was also a call for a UK/European equivalent to the Digital Cinema Lab set up by the Entertainment Technology Centre (ETC) in Hollywood. These two elements came together in the DTB.

The Test Bed is funded by the DTI, with support from the British Film Institute (BFI) and members of the film and technology industry that have contributed their equipment and/or time and expertise. These include Barco Digital Systems, Christie Digital, Denon, Digital Projection International, Digital Theatre Systems Dolby, JVC, Panastereo, Panasonic, QuVis, Screen Digest, Snell & Wilcox, SohoNet, Sony and Texas Instruments. The NFT is an ideal location to house the Test Bed because of its history, impartiality and high level of cinema expertise, as well as connections with the British and international film industry.

The objectives of the project are as follows, and initially the project will run for two years although it is expected that there will be a need for this

Objective 1

To build and operate a D-cinema Test facility to demonstrate all elements of digital cinema distribution and reproduction. This will enable experiments and investigations to be carried out on various parts of the D-cinema chain to gather data for the world standardization of parameters in D-cinema.

Objective 2

To produce reports on the experiments/investigations as output to the various D-cinema standardization bodies.

Objective 3

To offer equipment and systems suppliers the means of developing and testing new equipment and technology.

Objective 4

To offer content creators the opportunity to understand and adopt new E-/D-cinema concepts.

Objective 5

To produce a website to help disseminate the information gathered in the experiments and investigations. This site will be updated on, at least, a 14-day cycle.

Objective 6

To create awareness and understanding within the cinema and equipment industry through consultation, demonstration and dissemination of information.

Source: Boyd, R and Trigg, S (2000) Digital Test Bed Objectives. Bid Document, National Film Theatre

facility for some time and further funding will be sought from other potential funding partners.

The Test Bed will test and explore every aspect of the emerging technology of digital creation, distribution and exhibition of film, as well as other forms of alternative content. There is considerable work to be done in areas such as standardization, training and education and the Test Bed will provide a forum for debate for the industry. There are also new areas, such as interactivity, that are only in the early stages of development. The subject of the audiences' response to digital display has also only been marginally explored and the NFT and Test Bed will be presenting digitalized classics to its audience throughout 2004, as part of a Digital Futures programme, and finding out what these audiences think about the various issues regarding digital cinema.

The project will work with creatives, cinema exhibitors and technology providers and, not least, the audience to help make the transition from 35 mm film for cinema display to digital projection an improved experience that benefits all parties. In doing so, it is envisaged that the Test Bed will work with similar projects around the world, such as those in Japan, Brazil and Europe. Not least it is envisaged that it will work with the Entertainment Technology Centre (ETC) in Hollywood and the European Digital Cinema Forum (EDCF).

There are several projects and events that the DTB is scheduled to perform in its initial two year existence in order to reach its objectives. These range from holding seminars on the various aspects of digital, under-taking demonstrations of new technologies, carrying out standards and technology tests and comparisons, and exploring interactive possibilities. Some of the most recent events are an HD TV event to educate television producers about the use of HD, a Screen Digest Seminar on the alternative uses of digital cinema technology and demonstrations and tests of the 4K prototype from NTT in Japan, as well as other pieces of equipment. January 2004 saw the first seminar for archivists, who were able to explore the possibilities of digitalizing their collections, and a workshop for projectionists will introduce them to the technology that they could soon be using.

The Test Bed is equipped with the most advanced cinema technology in the world used for digital distribution, storage and projection. This includes several different projectors from different manufacturers (Barco, Christie, Digital Projection International) and using different technologies (Texas Instruments' DLP Cinema® and JVC's D-ILA), servers, routers, up-converters and most digital tape and disc formats, as well as digital audio and associated equipment.

The NFT plans to make use of the projection technology and capability of the Test Bed for its own film screenings throughout the life of the project. The HD digital projector means that any digitally originated film, whether a DV Dogma film or the latest Pixar animation, can be shown in its original and intended format. As more and more films take the digital route – whether shot on mini-DV, 24p high-definition (HD) cameras, digital intermediate (DI) or computer generated imagery and animation – they will no longer have to be transferred to 35 mm prints to be screened. Films can be shown off tape, DVDs, hard drives or piped in over cable or satellite. Older films from archives can also be re-mastered in digital and screened repeatedly without the copy getting scratched or worn over time. Most recently the Test Bed facility has enabled the NFT to host ResFest (November 2003) – an international digital film festival for new and established filmmakers. The test bed was used during the 2003 London Film Festival and will be used for all of the NFT festivals in 2004/05.

The DTB will work with organizations such as the UK Film Council, Skillset, the British Kinematograph Sound and Television Society (BKSTS) and the DTI, as well as international agencies such as the EDCF, SMPTE (the Society of Motion Picture and Television Engineers) and DCI (Digital Cinema Initiatives), and act as a catalyst for the dissemination of information about this technology across the industry. It is envisaged that the NFT will contribute towards the new Digital Screen Network (set up by the UK Film Council), which will enable it to reach new and wider audiences, particularly with education events and their Guardian Interviews, which are restricted to audiences on the South Bank.

Equipment

There are several key manufacturers whose equipment is vital to the Test Bed and the following explains the equipment specifications and purpose. One of the highlights of the Test Bed has been the positive working relationship that has developed between the various manufacturers and the quality of work being produced is testament to this. Most notably technical support from Rex Becket and David Monk from Texas Instruments have proved invaluable, as well as support from Peter Wilson from projector manufacturers Snell & Wilcox, and not least the NFT projection team.

Snell & Wilcox

The Test Bed has several pieces of Snell and Wilcox equipment in the engineering area. The equipment is there to facilitate conversion from the random formats that may be required to be shown and the Digital Cinema Projector heads that tend to be less flexible in formats than their regular counterparts. The equipment is as follows.

HD source   This is essentially a multi-purpose test pattern and reference generator. There are many variances in the image parameters for digital cinema and large screen projection in general. The HD source is used for systems test and as a reference device; it can generate a wide variety of digital formats.

Interpolator   The Interpolator is a very high-end Home Theatre video processor box. It is particularly optimized to take the output of a DVD player and convert the image for the best quality projection.

HD5100   The HD5100 is a professional up-converter with broadcast level digital inputs and outputs. It has the possibility of running as a simple up-converter or with an informed operator as a piece of laboratory equipment where conversion settings can be changed to allow evaluation of different source or display technology.

UKON The UKON is a professional quality general purpose converter. It can up-convert standard definition to higher resolutions, down-convert from higher to lower resolutions or temporally convert to the same resolution but running at a different speed, e.g. 1080i 59.94 to 1080p 24. Interlace to progressive conversion is also possible, from for example 1080i 59.94 to 720p 59.94, as is image size conversion (Aspect Ratio).

The digital cinema projectors are progressive scan devices so any incoming interlace formats need to be converted before display, e.g. $720 \times 576 \times 50I$ (PAL) to $2048 \times 1080 \times 25p$ (2K 25 fps).

Sound

The Digital Test Bed is equipped with three digital cinema ready sound systems provided by Dolby (CP650), Digital Theatre Systems (XD10 cinema media player) and Panastereo. Over the next 12 months the Test Bed will run a seminar on digital cinema sound and examine the issues surrounding digital cinema and other formats used in electronic projection.

QuVis

As a self-contained fully integrated unit comprising a full encoder and decoder, the QuBit is very flexible and cost effective for limited screenings. At the launch of the Test Bed the QuBit was used for demonstrating a/b comparisons with projected 35 mm film; the material used was from *The Insider*. The QuBit has also been used for screening various remastered Hollywood films such as *Singin' in the Rain, Casablanca* and *The Adventures of Robin Hood*.

An interesting demonstration of the QuBit's flexibility occurred when The Worx Digital, working with Anthony Minghella's company Mirage, took a work-in-progress from a Final Cut Pro system at standard definition resolutions and using Snell and Wilcox's up-conversion technology, up-converted the material at the Test Bed in real time to a discerning audience of industry professionals. This demonstrated yet another diverse use of the digital cinema system, and the feedback to Anthony Minghella and Walter Murch from the audience was invaluable in helping them understand the timing and pacing of the movie.

The QuBit server is a vital part of the Test Bed and one of several servers that will be used throughout the duration of the project. Negotiations are currently under way with EVS to use their MPEG-2 server to encode some of the films in the NFT's Digital Futures programming and at some point the Test Bed will invite other server manufacturers/providers to participate in an event whereby they can demonstrate their equipment.

Texas Instruments

It is the TI technology that has been the main driving force for the advancement of digital cinema technology to date. Their Digital Light Processor (DLP) is a digital micro-mirror device in which a number of individually movable mirrors reflect light from a lamp through a projector lens to form the image on screen. This DLP technology is used by the Christie and Barco projectors, which are the first projectors to be used by the Test Bed.

The Projectors

There are three main manufacturers for DLP projectors – Barco, Christie and Digital Projection International (DPI) – and all three are part of the Test Bed project. The Barco projector used is the DP50 with RC567 touch screen control, ×1.5 and ×1.9 anamorphic lenses to enable the highest resolution flat and wide screen format display and an Alternative Content Switcher and Router (ACSAR). The Christie projectors used is the DCP-H projector. This delivered a high contrast display of over 1350:1 and offers complete compatibility with 720-line and 1080-line HDTV standards. The DPI projector being used is the IS10, which has comparable technology to the Barco and Christie.

JVC has produced an alternative digital cinema technology in its D-ILA QX1 projector – the only other alternative to TI's DLP technology at this point. This technology is not aimed at the general exhibition industry; however, JVC are now currently working with Kodak in a joint venture to produce a projector that will cater to this industry sector. As participants in the Test Bed, JVC have brought in their projector for special events as a means to test and compare varying digital cinema technology.

7.3   European DocuZone (EDZ), *By Kees Ryninks and Bjorn Koll*

Introduction

The American studios are expected to set their standards for so-called D-cinema in 2004 (see Chapter 9). Even then it will take them between 5 and 10 years to equip all their cinemas for digital release. Of course, they will not equip the independent cinemas, which are so crucial for the European film culture. These will come under even greater pressure. At present we have a unique opportunity to create a digital network, which could become crucial for the survival of European Independent cinema. The nature of digital distribution and exhibition, with its flexibility in programming and cost-effectiveness in terms of release, makes it the perfect tool for reaching wider audiences for the small, specialized films which are so characteristic of European film culture.

Expanding on the Dutch DocuZone concept, which started digital distribution and exhibition in 10 cinemas in February 2002, the Netherlands Film Fund, in collaboration with German distributor Salzgeber & Co. Medien GmbH, developed a business model for a pan-European digital network, starting its operation in the second half of 2004. As the documentary genre is on the rise it was not difficult to find other countries to join. Although European DocuZone will start of as a network for documentaries, we envisage that it will also be used for shorts, animation and for low-budget features. It is a system made for the future, as digital cinema *is* the future and could become the saviour of the European film industry.

European DocuZone (EDZ) is the first digital distribution and exhibition network across eight European countries specifically intended for specialized European films. EDZ will facilitate the pan-European exchange of films and offers a platform for promotional collaboration. It brings together the experience and enthusiasm of producers, distributors and theatre-owners working together to create a new chance for our European film culture in order to survive the overwhelming influx of American movies. The EDZ partners in Austria, France, Germany, the Netherlands, Portugal, Spain, Scotland and Slovakia have the objective to distribute 12 European documentaries and trailers simultaneously into 200+ European cinemas, followed by live discussion via satellite links with directors after the show. On a local level the partners will organize additional screenings with other documentaries in their respective cinemas.

In order to achieve this goal EDZ will act as a post-production coordinator and will guarantee to high standards the subtitling of 12 European documentaries, image and sound compression, encryption and quality control. By supplying our own Cinema Servers to the participating cinemas, EDZ will deliver to European art house cinemas both a soft- and hardware tool offering data security, local and remote system monitoring, maintenance, control and automation.

The progress of the EDZ project is monitored, adjusted by and embedded in audience and promotional research by the UK based Docspace initiative to gather first hand information on target audiences especially interested in European documentaries and to exchange experiences between the European partners to maximize the project's success. EDZ will also supply an online documentary database for programming of documentaries to guarantee easier access to and exchange of films with an international appeal.

Working Together across Borders

EDZ is a combination of individual autonomous DocuZones which can make use of the facilities EDZ offers. All will have a minimum of 100 slots per year for domestic and foreign films, so most of those will be European. They have agreed to combine their effort in marketing and publicity campaigns, thus making further cost reductions possible. It will also make the sector as a whole more competitive within the industry through overall cost savings and centralized facilities: they will know their target audience through research, find their product through the database, adjust themselves to the market requirements and bring good quality, European product to the cinemas in areas where this product normally is hardly seen. EDZ will turn every theatre into a première (first run) theatre so anyone, anywhere can see a film in the first week, when the publicity campaigns are at their strongest.

Euro Docs

One of the most exciting prospects of having a pan-European network is the easier exchange of films with an international appeal. Each participating DocuZone can offer one or two documentaries per year for general, international release. If sufficient countries would like to include this documentary in their programme, then EDZ will encode and encrypt it, and marry it with the subtitling files provided by each country. The final product will be sent via satellite to all theatres in the network. The revenues (after deduction of basic costs) will be passed to the local DocuZone and subsequently to the producers. Of course the same applies for distributors with rights outside their own territory. The network gives them easier access to foreign theatres.

Central Co-ordination of European Programming

The amount of pan-European programming is defined as 12 documentaries in the first year, plus four pan-European cultural events, such as pan-European opening nights of festivals, Award ceremonies or selected short film programmes. A certain amount of screenings could also be agreed with commercial partners, such as record companies for the promotion of their latest DVD. Each local DocuZone will have its own programme co-ordinator who is responsible for liaising with the central organization and for selecting the best pan-European documentaries. Our ambition is to extend the programming to shorts, animation and low-budget features.

Central Play-out Centre

In developing the business model we decided that the simplest and economically most viable model would be one in which the equipment, technical back-up and technical facilities would be dealt with within one centralized organization. This will be Salzgeber, a well-known German distributor in Berlin. They will equip a play-out centre suitable for digitalizing, encoding and encrypting the chosen documentaries and transmitting them via satellite to the local DocuZones.

One Standardized Server-based System

Our business model is based on the premise that one standardized satellite/ server system is the crucial element if one wants to exchange European programming. All server systems in the 200+ cinemas will be the same and use the same software. EuroDocs and other films that distributors want to distribute internationally could be supplied to the central play-out centre on DigiBeta or HD tapes. There they will be encoded and encrypted to MPEG2 HD level and married with different subtitling files to be distributed via satellite to all theatres in the network. Digital Rights Management and data protection will be offered at the highest standard currently available.

Other Features

Local DocuZones

Each country will have its own local DocuZone infrastructure, which will be responsible for the co-ordination of domestic programming, subtitling, marketing and publicity. The local DocuZone is also responsible for liaising with the central play-out centre in Germany and as such will become a technical sub-station. Here domestic product can be prepared for delivery to the local theatres either via satellite or ATM data links or on standard videotapes or DVD for cost-effective distribution.

The local DocuZones can be organized in the way that is best suited for the needs and budgets of the individual countries. That is why the responsibility for raising the local funds lies with those DocuZones. The local DocuZones could be a one-person operation, an extra task for an established distributor, a voluntary organization or a state-financed distributor, which could also deal with shorts and specialized features.

Central Database

One of the biggest problems in programming regular weekly slots is the difficulties in getting master tapes and viewing tapes of foreign product on time for the release. Though it is in the interest of producers, distributors and sales agents to send their documentaries out on request it still remains a weak spot in the chain of (digital) distribution. It is for this reason that EDZ will incorporate one central database where master and viewing tapes are stored and where a tape can be requested to be sent by satellite to a receiver-unit.

In the future every local DocuZone will be able to access the catalogued viewing tapes, which would save them tremendous costs in labour and transport. It will guarantee that all DocuZones will have access to the best documentaries available (and possibly later independent feature films).

Central Audience Monitoring and Market Research

Digital technology will change the bottom line of documentary exhibition to make documentary programming for the big screen economically viable. To assess the effects of the EDZ initiative we have incorporated in the overall strategy the DocSpace research project to create a comprehensive, on-going overview on European documentary audiences. This survey will start in June 2004 and will monitor at regular intervals till December 2005 the effects of different programming and promotion on documentary audiences across the member European countries. In this way programming and promotional campaigns can be adjusted accordingly. They will report back to the programme co-ordinators every three months, closing with a conference in 2006 for the European film industry.

Other Distributors and Access

EDZ is not just for the members of the organizations. The network is open to any distributor wanting to release specialized product. This in turn will mean that distributors are more willing to take risks with those films as their initial outlay for release is much lower. They can make use of all the facilities provided to the DocuZone members. Again this will mean more competitiveness within the Zone, but it also means that any serious distributor can become more competitive against the influence from other genres and other continents.

Pan-European Events

EDZ will make it possible to turn every première into an event, and we know from festival attendance figures that audiences want to meet like-minded people in the theatres. Directors can introduce their films Europe-wide across 200+ screens and Q&As can be held via live links. We can see that recent European documentaries can bring back their audience to the theatres: the French *Etre et Avoir* attracted over two million visitors in France alone and Norway's *Cool & Crazy* reached more than one million in the Scandinavian countries. The audience is out there and we will bring them out of their homes and into the cinemas.

Professional Expertise

The most important guarantee we can give that this project will succeed is the group of professionals it has working together. They have between them more than 200 years of experience. They have come together driven by the desire to find new outlets for their films, which they know are good but for which there is now little space in the theatres. They are compassionate and eager to make it work. But it is not just about passion. They are also keen businessmen who run successful companies or are in influential positions. They see EDZ as their last and only chance to make an impact on the market and they will continue to make it happen, together and across the borders of the past – for themselves, for European filmmakers and, most importantly, for European audiences.

Acknowledgement

I wish to acknowledge Bjorn Koll of Salzgeber & Co. Medien GmbH and Amy Hardie of DocSpace Ltd, my close collaborators in the founding of EDZ.

European DocuZone is a Netherlands Film Fund initiative with the support of the MEDIA PLUS programme of the European Community.

7.4   **Folkets Hus Digital Houses Project,** *By Lasse Svanberg*

Background

Folkets Hus & Parker (FHP) is a Swedish non-governmental movement with links to the labour movement. In the early 1930s they started building special houses, Folkets Hus, all over Sweden, intended for meetings, lectures, theatre, concerts, cinema etc. Most of these houses were placed in small or medium-sized towns in the rural parts of Sweden and approximately half of them were equipped with cinemas, so-called multi-purpose cinemas.

FHP is today Sweden's largest cinema owner in quantitative terms, with 267 cinemas and 53 958 seats. Most cinemas are single-screens with 200–250 seats and an average screen-width of 6 m. The FHP cinema chain is, however, quite small in financial terms, accounting for 3–4% of Sweden's total box office. In 2000 the management realized that they faced a choice of either closing down many of the old, non-profitable cinemas or investing in new technology. They decided on the latter. A pilot project, Digitala Hus (Digital Houses), was launched on 30 August 2002 in seven locations in northern and central Sweden. This was the first digital cinema network of its kind in Europe.

The Digital Houses

At an early stage the FHP management realized that E-cinema (and D-cinema) means more than just digitalizing traditional cinemas; the biggest challenge lies in creating an entirely new form of public venue (or hall) with the help of present-day digital display and telecommunications technology and local community commitment. The traditional 'cinema' concept tends to block the view ahead towards what E-cinema can develop into in the near future (not least for traditional, commercial cinema operators). This is why the project was called Digital Houses, not Digital Cinemas.

FHP also realized that digital film distribution and film exhibition technology would make it possible for their rural cinemas to receive first release films much earlier than before, and in much better technical condition. Previously they had to wait for weeks (sometimes months) before a new popular film had been shown in the bigger cities and they could get hold of a print – and that print was often full of dirt, scratches and splices after its big city tour.

The Digital Houses network today consists of eight cinemas (4000 seats) with five new sites being installed at the end of 2004 (most of them in southern Sweden). The projectors used are Barco DP 30 and DP 100 plus a couple of Barco dark-chip DLPs. EVS Cinestore Server, Barco Pictor compression, Cinea encryption and EVS subtitling have been installed. Live satellite transmission is received through 100 cm satellite dishes and Wegener 401 Receivers (encrypted signals PAL, stereo, 4:3 and 16:9), in cooperation with Teracom and NSAB/SIRIUS. Together with KTH (Royal Institute of Technology), broadband fibre-optic network connections have been established capable of uncompressed HD signal transmissions at 1.5 Gb levels. The Digital Houses are also interconnected by a closed circuit network.

The audience reactions to this new way of watching films have been very positive: they appreciate having brand new films on the screen (simultaneously with big city releases), rock-steady clear images, no dirt, scratches or other typical film artefacts. A tremendous step forward in terms of image quality, and at a level just below 1.3K resolution! Attendance and revenues in the first seven Digital Houses rose by 25–30% during 2003 (compared to the previous non-digital year). Seventeen Swedish feature films and four international features got their first releases in Digital Houses. Screening of new Hollywood films is still on the negotiation table and will probably not be solved until an international technical standard for D-cinema is established. Several deals have however, already been made with independent studios in the United States.

Digital Film

With regard to digital film prints, Scandinavia's major film laboratory, FilmTeknik in Stockholm (www.filmteknik.se) has installed the necessary equipment for digital film print production. They are produced from D5, D6 or HDCAM masters and stored on LTO data-tape 200 Gb cartridges. Every Digital House gets a copy of its own (with a personal encrypted code) which is then loaded into the server. They can keep their digital print as long as they like (or can make money from it), without having to rush it on to some other cinema prematurely. The cost for a digital master is approx. 2600 Euro, a single digital print (including master cost) is 600 Euro. If 20 prints are made the cost per print will be as low as 230 Euro (compared to 2200 Euro for a 35 mm release print).

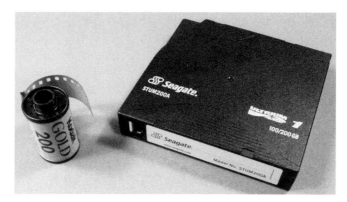

Fig 7.1   Digital feature film print FHP style: LTO data-tape cartridge (photo: Lasse Svanberg).

Other Content

The Digital Houses are, of course, also showing 35 mm (celluloid) films and are well equipped for showing alternative (non-film) content. Broadway shows have been shown digitally, a David Bowie concert and a stage production of *Les Miserables* live via satellite and in co-operation with European partners, to mention just a few alternative content examples. The latest project is a deal with EURO 1080, Europe's first HDTV channel serving, among others, E-cinemas. This means a continuous outlet for rock concerts, operas, theatre and live sports in HD quality and Dolby 5.1 Surround sound through the Digital Houses (plus another 'black box' in the screening room – a Tandberg receiver, TT1282 HD professional receiver).

Finance

The project has no government funding, but has, however, lately received limited support from the Swedish Film Institute for the production of digital prints. Financing comes chiefly from FHP itself and the labour movement, plus very important contributions from municipalities and local companies. And, of course, ticket sales.

Future Possibilities

A digital network of this kind offers interesting new opportunities for young digital filmmakers and for local digital film production. This possibility has not been fully explored yet, the only example being a snow-boarding film called *Stomped*, produced on DV-CAM by a group of youngsters in northern Sweden, edited on Macintosh home computers and screened in all Digital Houses from DigiBeta cassettes.

Further information on the Digital Houses project is available from Rickard Gramfors, rickard.gramfors@fhp.nu.

7.5   UK Film Council Digital Projects, *By Peter A. Packer*

The UK Film Council

Film is an immensely powerful medium at the heart of the UK's creative industries within the global economy. The UK Film Council is the government's strategic agency for film in the UK, ensuring that the economic, cultural and educational aspects of film are effectively represented at home and abroad. Set up in April 2000, the UK Film Council invests government grant-in-aid and National Lottery money in a targeted way and aims to deliver lasting benefits to the public and the industry.

UK Film Council has also co-funded and helped to set up nine new regional screen agencies which complement the policies and strategies of the UK Film Council by developing film at a regional level. The agencies invest significantly in training, nurturing new talent, developing local industry such as digital production. The UK Film Council also works with the national film agencies for Scotland (see www.scottishscreen.com), Wales (see www.sgrin.co.uk) and Northern Ireland (see www.niftc.co.uk).

Encouraging people to engage with film throughout their lives is central to the UK Film Council's aims for developing film culture in the UK. An innovative initiative to get young people involved in film was established through setting up First Light young people from all backgrounds across the UK make their own films using new digital technologies (see www.first-lightmovies.com). The British Film Institute (*bfi*), the UK Film Council's principal partner in education and access, continues to be funded to deliver a wide range of digital and other initiatives, including the innovative 'screenonline' project outlined below (see also www.bfi.org.uk).

The UK Film Council's first three years were focused on restructuring the public money it has available to support the effect development of scripts and the financing of new British films. The organisation is now focusing on tackling issues which are key to the longer-term development of a sustainable film industry and a vibrant film culture. The principles are outlined in Sir Alan Parker's 2002 presentation *Building a sustainable UK film industry* (see www.ukfilmcouncil.org.uk then downloads.) Realizing this vision involves the industry moving forward on three main fronts:

- Integrating the UK film production sector much more closely with effective distribution.
- Enhancement of the UK's globally competitive skills base.
- Enhancement of our world-class infrastructure of studios and production and post-production facilities.

The Challenge of Digital Technology

One of the key areas for activity and over the next three years for the UK Film Council is the field of digital technology which, with all the new challenges and associated risks, obviously has very great significance for the increasingly inter-related areas of both production and distribution and exhibition.

Digital technology is redefining film and the UK must equip itself accordingly. This is a time of transition and various, often conflicting, factors can be detected at work. For example, the rapid evolution of products and processes means that the development cycle is swift. High research and development costs are followed by a rapid lowering of unit prices and then by obsolescence. There are well-identified risks involved in being 'first to market' which are holding back progress, particularly in key areas such as distribution and exhibition.

A recent position paper has outlined the UK Film Council's initial thinking in this area (see www.ukfilmcouncil.org.uk then downloads). The UK Film Council will also continue to host occasional seminars to enable professionals to share knowledge, information and best practice to assist competitiveness and to maximize the creative and learning potential of new technology. At the same time it continues to invest in digital production and for the first time will also invest in digital film distribution and exhibition. The UK Film Council is also investigating the possibilities of a new partnership with Arts Council England to support visual artists and experimental filmmakers working creatively with digital technology.

Four areas of the UK Film Council's current and future policy and activities are especially relevant here:

- The New Cinema Fund – pushing the boundaries in new technologies and creativity
- *bfi* screenonline – using digital technologies to develop and inform the audiences of the future
- The UK Film Skills Strategy – building a workforce for tomorrow
- Distribution and Exhibition Fund – using new technologies to transform the environment

This chapter will now look at each initiative in turn.

New Cinema Fund

By the end of 2003, the New Cinema Fund had made some 30 feature film awards and awards to third parties to run a variety of shorts funding schemes producing 200 short films so far. The total value of the feature film awards made was almost 14 million pounds. Projects included *Bloody Sunday* (winner of the Golden Bear, Berlin 2002), *The Magdalene Sisters* (winner of the Golden Lion, Venice 2002), and *Noi the Albino* (winner of The Nordic Film Award, Goteburg 2003). Expenditure for the three years starting April 2004 will run at 5 million pounds per year.

Above all, the New Cinema Fund continues to support creativity, innovation, new talent and 'cutting edge' filmmaking. It has an especially strong commitment to supporting work from the English regions, to stimulating diversity in the output of the production sector and, through initiatives such as the Berlinale Talent Campus, to equip UK filmmakers to operate more effectively across Europe. The Fund supports films and filmmakers whose work demonstrates passion and verve and whose films aim to connect with a broad range of audiences.

With its fervent desire to push the boundaries in both digital technologies and innovation the New Cinema Fund seeks and explores unique and groundbreaking projects. For example, *This Is Not A Love Song* was the New Cinema Fund's first digital feature film designed specifically to take advantage of new production and distribution methods. On 5 September 2003, *This Is Not A Love Song* became the world's first online E-première, with a simultaneous theatrical release across the UK. The film, directed by Bille Eltringham (*The Darkest Light*) and written by Simon Beaufoy (*The Full Monty*), is a taught thriller set against the vast landscape of the Northern Moors. Using the techniques and immediacy of digital filmmaking, the film follows two petty criminals who become killers as they attempt to escape cross-country to the safety of the city before a posse of vengeful farmers can hunt them down.

The event received major UK and international exposure. It was marketed and promoted by both NTL and BT Openworld and generated 246 separate editorial placements on 244 websites across the UK. In its first day on release the film made headline news on BBC Breakfast, 6pm and 10pm news in addition to several radio stations across the UK. Online it made front-page news at CNN.com, reached Google's Top Ten – surpassing all expectations – and in its opening weekend received over 175 000 hits.

The film was encrypted and securely encoded to be made available online within UK borders only until 24 September 2003. Customers were charged per download onto a PC only via credit card. In tandem with the online release of 5 September, *This Is Not A Love Song* received a (UK-wide) theatrical release that stretched from London to Edinburgh. Distributed by Soda Pictures the film was also digitally projected and exclusively streamed to an audience at the Watershed Cinema, Bristol. *This Is Not A Love Song* was then booked to be screened further in cinemas across the UK from January 2004.

The next feature to be released, Simon Pummel's *Bodysong*, was distributed by Pathé. *Bodysong* is a story compiled from 100% digital archive footage and has been scored by Jonny Greenwood from Radiohead.

The New Cinema Fund searches for new and upcoming talent with its UK-wide Digital Shorts Scheme, which is the largest scheme of its kind in the world. In addition, a new avenue of shorts distribution has also been established. Customers at more than 500 leading hair salons across the UK now have an alternative to thumbing their way through old magazines, thanks to a new initiative which has allowed them to watch short films from Britain's hottest young filmmakers using the very latest in interactive digital technology. Handled by Short Circuit and in co-operation with digital media owner I-VU, since August 2003 clients at selected hair salons all over the UK have been able to use interactive audiovisual touch screens to access the latest cutting-edge short films.

bfi screenonline

The UK Film Council's key partner the British Film Institute is actively developing a wide range of digital initiatives (see www.bfi.org.uk), the newest of which and a very significant venture in terms of access and media literacy, is an exciting new digital venture, *bfi* screenonline. This will be a free online film resource in UK public libraries and schools.

bfi screenonline offers a guide to Britain's rich and diverse moving image history, giving access to material preserved in the *bfi* National Film and Television Archive. The service comprises initially up to 1000 hours of digitized moving image material, thousands of still images, hundreds of scripts and posters from the *bfi*'s collections, with in-depth contextual information on all aspects of British film and television history. Teachers, students and general users will be able to directly access the resource which might be developed still further to meet other key educational and cultural objectives.

UK Film Skills Strategy

A sustainable industry needs a skilled workforce. To this end, the UK Film Council has significantly increased its commitment to skills training to nearly £6.5 million a year from April 2004 to support the first comprehensive skills strategy for film across the UK.

There are initiatives to raise awareness of new technologies and software, including the capabilities and limitations of digital technologies. This new strategy (see *A Bigger Picture: The UK Film Skills Strategy* published by the UK Film Council and Skillset, the UK Sector Skills Council for the Audio Visual Industries) (www.skillset.org) aims to assess the value of sector specific workshops dealing with digital technology to provide an open debate and help the industry anticipate the effects it will have on the film business, and identify skills gaps and shortages.

In 2001 the Skillset/DCMS Audio Visual Industries Training Group (AVITG) report 'Skills for Tomorrow's Media' recommended that, '*The BBC should explore, as soon as possible, the feasibility of setting up an online training facility for audio visual workers.*' In response to this recommendation, and in support of this UK Film Skills Strategy, BBC Training and Development has collaborated with Skillset to develop a pilot for the provision of online training, beginning with content relating to High Definition (HD) technologies. The lessons learned from this pilot will be used to inform the development of further content. It is envisaged that Skillset will work with the BBC infrastructure to provide film-specific online educational packages and opportunities.

Looking ahead, it has become clear that in order to assist the creation of a favourable environment for film in the UK, the UK Film Council must properly resource training and skills for the industry distribution and exhibition for audiences of 'specialized' films and selected smaller British films (see Distribution and Exhibition Fund, below). In both cases the UK Film Council has no option. The private sector, left to its own devices, cannot meet these considerable challenges and there is a clear rationale for a publicly funded intervention.

A sustainable industry needs a skilled workforce…

Distribution and Exhibition Fund

In association with Arts Council England, the UK Film Council has committed over 20 million pounds to improve significantly the circulation and enjoyment of specialized cinema in the UK as well as supporting a wider release of selected commercially attractive smaller British films.

It is both a matter of fact and regret that audiences in the UK are less adventurous than their counterparts in Europe. Consequently, specialized distribution and exhibition in the UK is a small, fragile and risky business sector which struggles to grab visibility for its product in the face of the mainstream, commercial film sector. Given this, the UK Film Council's key objectives are:

- To ensure that a broader and more diverse range of films is available for audiences to view across the UK.
- To develop audience appreciation, enjoyment and understanding of film.
- To increase audience uptake of specialized films and thereby help increase levels of cinema-going in the UK.
- To provide greater opportunities for disabled people (particularly audiences with sensory impairments) to access and enjoy cinema.
- To encourage exhibitors, distributors and broadcasters to engage more fully with a diversity of audiences and to value the longer term goals of audience development.

A number of initiatives were developed after detailed consultation with the industry during 2001 and 2002 to put in place a ground-breaking digital exhibition and distribution programme. Public funding was allocated in the form of 3 million pounds a year from the UK Film Council and a total of 15 million pounds from Arts Council England. The key components are:

- A capital fund for the creation of a Digital Screen Network using high-specification digital equipment for the wider exhibition of specialized film in all types of cinemas across the UK.
- A Specialised Prints and Advertising (P&A) Fund to support the wider release and exploitation of specialized films.
- A UK Film Distribution Programme to underwrite the wider release of new British films with significant commercial potential.
- A fund for a pilot project in cinemas providing equipment to project soft-titles onto regular screening prints for the benefit of people with hearing impairments, equipment to transmit on-screen action descriptions for people with visual impairments, support for the production of more subtitled copies of films on limited release and a research fund to assess future needs and requirements of cinemagoers with sensory impairments.
- A fund for digital equipment for film societies and mobile cinema operators to increase access to films in rural and remote geographical areas.
- A fund for small scale capital building and renovation projects.
- A fund for educational activities aimed at improving knowledge of film and cinema.

Digital Screen Network

Given the UK Film Council's key objectives in relation to distribution and exhibition, outlined above, digital technology offers the opportunity for a ground-breaking step-change in this sector of the industry. Several factors are currently limiting or inhibiting the wide and efficient dissemination of specialized films. These include the high cost of distribution, especially of prints, and the limited number of outlets where they might play. Curtailed playing time and limited audiences in turn restrict the films' commercial prospects, especially as they generally receive restricted coverage by the media and afterwards limited TV uptake by mainstream channels. The fragmented co-ordination of releases across territories is also a barrier to wider public enjoyment of specialized films.

Using digital technology will lower the cost of entry into the market via lower print and physical distribution costs and also achieve wider availability of film choice. More cinemas can show 'specialized' films and the booking and programming of such will become more flexible. In this way the traditional distribution/exhibition model is changed and the landscape radically altered for specialized films.

In broad outline, the UK Film Council's Digital Screen Network (DSN) Distribution and Exhibition Strategy is to digitalize up to 250 screens in approximately 150 cinemas, with UK-wide coverage. All types of cinemas, e.g. existing specialized, publicly supported, multiplex, independent, etc., will be eligible for inclusion using the highest possible level of equipment and technology (e.g. Texas Instruments' 2K DLP Cinema projectors with the latest servers and encryption technology). Technical standards will be the highest possible at the point of entry and will be as close to DCI (Digital Cinema Initiatives) standards as appropriate for the initiative (see Chapter 9).

In terms of the programming strategy the films will generally be booked via the normal distributor/exhibitor relationship. The UK Film Council will have a number of centrally booked programming 'slots' for one-off screenings of film with an emphasis on education, archive, day-and-date premières, etc. Additional programming may include local productions, shorts, film club screenings, mini film festivals, etc.

Efforts are also being made to encourage independent producers to deliver an HD digital master as part of their normal deliverables to sales agents and/or distributors. This will allow greater access of their films to a much wider audience in the UK. At present, digital mastering is often only done to DigiBeta level which is arguably not adequate for theatrical exhibition. The cost differential between the two levels at post-production stage is marginal when compared to the cost involved in re-mastering directly from 35 mm. An HD digital master can then also be used throughout the world as it only needs to be produced once.

As part of its overall Digital Screen Network strategy, the UK Film Council will work with the industry to ensure that front-end scanning and mastering, compression, encryption and physical delivery media services exist at affordable prices to act as an additional incentive for distributors to fully engage with the project.

The marketing strategy will be crucial and will seek to develop a brand for the Digital Screen Network itself and for specialized film as a genre and give the whole sector a more public face. This will be achieved in conjunction with major media partners (press and/or TV) via a new website, local press and radio, national press and local films clubs. All this will make a considerable addition to the routine activities of distributors and exhibitors in their normal publicity and advertising activities.

The UK Film Council believes its strategy will bring a number of overall benefits to the sector and principally that it will radically increase public access to specialized films and markedly increase the range of films on offer to the general public. The strategy is democratic and inclusive and would be open to the complete range of exhibitors and distributors. It is gaining overall industry acceptance because of the many benefits it will bring, quite apart from the additional advantage that it will open up possibilities also for the *bfi*'s and other archive materials to become more accessible. Continuing feedback from the industry and other key stakeholders will lead to refinement of the strategy.

Funding for relevant parts of the strategy is to come on a partnership basis, at point of take-up, from the distribution, exhibition and education sectors. Importantly, the UK Film Council is already in discussions with DCMS (the UK Department for Culture, Media and Sport) and ACE to plan the long term development of the Digital Screen Network.

Conclusion

Taken together, these practical and policy developments represent a considerable investment in, and commitment to, the challenges and opportunities of the digital industrial and cultural environment. The UK Film Council's interventions are designed to be strategic and long term: supporting the industry, promoting change, enabling the social and cultural effects of digitalization to be considered and explored alongside the technological ones and backing all these initiatives with sound research and the gathering of statistical information by its Research and Statistics Unit. These measures contribute to the UK Film Council's over-arching aim of building a competitive, vibrant UK film industry and a truly engaged and critical audience.

8

The Digital Future of Cinema – So Close, and Yet So Far Away

Patrick von Sychowski

As digital cinema reaches its fifth anniversary, the promise of a future with celluloid-free theatres appears as tantalizingly close as when *Star Wars*: *Episode I, The Phantom Menace* became the first ever film to be screened in digital to paying audiences in four US multiplexes in the summer of 1999. Yet, five years on just 250 screens world wide have been converted to cinema quality digital projection and celluloid continues to demonstrate the resilience that has seen 35 mm be the most universal and longest surviving audiovisual format of all time.

Over 120 films have been screened to regular cinemagoers in higher-end digital cinema multiplexes around the world. Most of these are Hollywood films, but an increasing number of local titles from Brazil, China and Sweden have started to appear in recent years. Several hundred more digital films have been screened at film festivals, in one-off special screenings, in non-film venues or on lower-end equipment, all using some form of digital projection. Satellite delivery, live streaming, HDTV events on cinema screens, all have been shown to work and to attract audiences in significant numbers.

So why is it that the large scale roll-out of digital cinema still appears to be just around the corner, as could have been said at any time in the past five years, not to mention at even earlier instances of (false) digital, HD or electronic cinema dawns?

Broadly speaking, there are four main criteria that digital cinema must fulfil in order to be ready for large scale deployment: technology, standards, business models and content. This chapter will examine each of these in turn and see whether the promise of an end-to-end digital chain is likely to be fulfilled any time soon at the projection end.

Technology

Over 10 years on from its first prototype presentation, and five years after the 'shoot out' contest that saw off its only serious challenger to date, Texas Instruments' DLP Cinema technology remains the king of the digital cinema projection technology hill. Rival technologies from the likes of JVC (the ILA/D-ILA light valve technology that was trounced by TI in 1999) remains too unaffordable and impractical, while Sony's GLV remains in the lab. Laser projection remains unattainable at affordable levels.

There can be no doubt that when the global digital cinema revolution happens, it will be reflected and projected off the millions of individually movable micro mirrors that form the heart of the DLP Cinema projectors. Yet it was not until TI demonstrated its so-called 2K projector (what TI calls the 'm25', with a 2048×1080 resolution) that the majority of exhibitors and studios declared themselves sufficiently happy with the quality level of the technology. There had previously been damaging criticisms of the DLP Cinema 1.3K/15m projectors having less resolution than HDTV home displays. TI's three OEM licensees Barco, Christie and DPI/NEC, began shipping 2K/m25 projectors in October of 2003, following significant initial orders from Kinepolis (Belgium), City Screen (UK), China Film Group (China) and Eng Wah (Singapore).

Attention on technology deficiencies of digital cinema now switched to servers and particularly the current choice between inadequate compression technology, based on open standards (such as MPEG-2), or higher quality from proprietary solutions (Qualcomm and QuVis). The aim is to find an 'open' higher-end compression algorithm for digital cinema along the lines of J-PEG 2000, 'Lite' version of which is the latest proposal mooted.

Security is at present less of an urgent concern than targeting off-screen camcorder piracy with watermarking techniques and leaked insider copies of films – as demonstrated by the 2004 Oscar 'screener' standoff between MPA and smaller distributors and trade bodies and critics' guilds (BAFTA, WGA, DGA, etc.). Yet any digital cinema system aiming for mass deployment will have to demonstrate significant security robustness.

Standards

The lengthy and complicated nature of the search for universal and open digital cinema standards, initiated by SMPTE DC28, has caught even seasoned insiders by surprise. The situation was complicated early on by the efforts of ITU (International Telecommunications Union) to mandate HDTV as the global digital cinema standard, a move that was fiercely resisted by the Hollywood studios.

Renewed impetus came from the formation by the seven Hollywood studios of Digital Cinema Initiatives LLC (DCI), a two-year joint venture set up to establish technical specifications for digital cinema, which all the studios could agree upon (see Chapter 9). DCI's mandate was set to expire in March 2004, when it was expected to deliver its final specification. It is being extended for a further few months, however, to take into account business issues raised by the two exhibitor trade bodies NATO and UNIC. These two had complained, in an open letter in December 2003, that too much was being done to resolve security issues (seemingly at the expense of cinema owners' control) and not enough on how to finance the roll-out.

International bodies such as the European Digital Cinema Forum (EDCF) and the Digital Cinema Consortium (DCC) of Japan are themselves not standard setting bodies, but provide forums for the members to have input on the global stage. With MPEG having been written off by Hollywood in the long term, five new compression standards are currently vying for approval in the evaluation tests going on in Hollywood in 2004. The approval of a compression solution will be the most important standard setting exercise that digital cinema will ever have to face.

Business Models

There is an unspoken understanding between studios and cinema owners that 35 mm print and distribution cost savings should and will ultimately help pay for the coming large scale digital cinema installations, coupled with the acknowledgement that exhibitors should also ultimately own the equipment.

This tacit 'agreement' has, however, not yet resulted in anything even approaching a formal agreement between distributors and exhibitors. NATO (National Association of Theatre Owners) has been involved in lengthy discussions with DCI, which has also held direct talks with exhibitors, while NATO has also been having direct meetings with the studios, to try to resolve this vexed issue. A widely touted proposal would be for some form of bonded lease, rather than (as previously mooted) involving a venture such as GE Capital. Assuming that standards have been agreed by early-to-mid 2004, NATO and DCI aim to have some form of business agreement worked out before the end of 2004.

Service Providers

Third-party digital cinema service providers such as Technicolor Digital Cinema (TDC) and Boeing Digital Cinema (BDC) have effectively fallen by the wayside while DCI and others are deliberating standards.

Having promised to 'seed' the US cinema market with 1000 installations in 2001, TDC laid off its Business Development and Exhibitor Relations department in 2002, though it continues to support existing installations. BDC was spun off from its parent company before in early 2004, though it was unclear until the last minute who might be interested in the unit. Both companies claimed that they would continue to be active in this space, but it appeared that a third generation of digital cinema service providers such as Dolby and Access Integrated Technologies (Access IT) by then stood a better chance of catering to any 'middle man' digital cinema needs. As it is to confirm this, Access IT acquired the assets of BDC in April 2004, having previously bought Hollywood Software, in its attempt to conquer the digital cinema market.

These third generation companies have carved out a service-provision niche for themselves in digital cinema that does not directly involve buying, installing and/or running projectors in cinemas, similarly to TDC and BDC. Dolby, for example, is using its Production Services division to become more involved at the exhibitor end, while the acquisition of DemoGraFX and Cinea signalled its intention for a greater role in, respectively, the front-end visual services sector and security. AccessIT has meanwhile effectively bought its way into the market with the acquisition of Hollywood Software and former management from TDC, as well as the assets of BDC. Kodak is meanwhile focusing on its Cinema Operating System (COS), promoted as good for digital pre-show advertising today and ideal for digital cinema tomorrow, which it is said to roll out to over 1,000 screens in US by September 2004.

If the second generation of digital cinema third-party players (TDC and BDC) over-reached themselves, the next generation is happier for a lower profile to fill the unavoidable gap in service provisions that digital distribution and exhibition of films creates.

International Ventures

Outside of the United States, both public and private ventures are pushing ahead with their own installation plans without waiting for DCI specifications. Partially publicly funded European efforts such as Folkets Hus (Sweden) and DocuZone (Netherlands) make do with standard DLP projectors, even though these are not deemed 'good enough' for first run, mainstream Hollywood content in digital. Consortium operators/integrators that do use DLP Cinema projectors, such as TeleImage in Brazil and T-Joy in Japan, have had to offer a lot of native titles to keep their digital-only screens occupied.

The two largest public digital cinema efforts as of early 2004 differ greatly in aim. China Film Groups has planned 100 installations for test bed evaluation – with one-third installed as of January 2004 – that is likely to lead ultimately to the development of native Chinese digital cinema solutions. The UK Film Council's 250-projector Digital Screen Network (DSN) planned for 2004 is aimed at enabling the greater distribution of specialized film, but is geared to the top-quality tier that would also enable it to screen Hollywood content in digital.

On the alternative end, there has been increased interest in combining cheap projectors with MPEG-4-based PC servers, used primarily for local or 'indie' films. Such efforts include Digital Cinema Solutions (USA), Rain Networks (Brazil) and H2DH (India). There were almost 150 lower-end digital projection solutions in smaller Indian towns and villages at the start of 2004, most of them installed by the Mukta Adlab-GDC joint venture.

Content

Of the four issues, content (that is, digital films) has so far proved the most difficult. The drip-drip supply of titles in digital by the Hollywood studios has meant that digital projectors have often stood dark for weeks or even months on end. Only Disney and Warner Bros have made any significant effort to release their titles in digital – lately joined by Fox – while the other studios have only screened one or two titles.

Any latent digital cinema title capacity that may result from the greater use of digital intermediate (DI) and digital source mastering (DSM) in post-production will soon have to materialize to back up whatever initiative DCI may propose in the wake of agreeing on any set of technical specification.

In the meantime, there has been a steadier output of local content in digital by several regional digital operators, often at a rate of one or more titles per month. These ventures include Folkets Hus (Sweden), TeleImage (Brazil), DocuZone (Holland), Arts Alliance/City Screen (UK), Mukta Adlab (India) and others, putting many a Hollywood studio to shame in comparison. Mukta Adlab alone released 36 titles in its first year of operation.

Conclusion

While it looks likely that all four criteria outlined above will imminently be met and overcome, digital cinema will ultimately depend on pressure for deployment coming from both exhibitors and studios. Neither has so far let themselves be rushed into digital (mainly by the hardware manufacturers' insistence that their technology works and should therefore be deployed).

It seems that ultimately the only 'market force' that will push both distributors and exhibitors is the increased reliance on worldwide, day-and-date, ultra-wide releases for major blockbusters and sequels, in the face of ever-more sophisticated digital piracy. The Technicolor and Deluxe film replication labs simply do not have enough printmaking capacity for a simultaneous global 30 000+ print release of *Harry Potter 4*.

If there is an early success story of digital display in cinemas, it is in the one field that has nothing to fear from piracy and is not lumbered with a high-end visual quality legacy. The greatest digital proliferation so far has been lower-end networked systems – projectors and plasma lobby displays – used for pre-film advertising in cinemas, with a dozen ventures active around the world on over 8000 screens as of mid 2004. While these are often dismissed as the poor relative of 'true' digital cinema technology, entrepreneurial operators have already seized the opportunities that the new equipment offers. In South Africa alone, five digital 'film' festivals were held in less than one year on standard definition electronic projectors costing a fraction of the 2K DLP Cinema kit, proving to the world that Hollywood will have to get its digital act together soon, unless it wants to see its gestating digital agenda scuppered in the rest of the world.

9

Standards

Peter Wilson

Why Do We Need Standards?

In the early days of the industrial revolution everything was bespoke. The pace of change was limited and the lack of tolerances meant everything had to be hand-fettled. One of the first items in engineering to be standardized was the screw thread.

In a museum near where I live there is a gun made by the Turks in 1464 to bombard the walls of Constantinople. The breech screws on to the barrel had a perfect screw thread. It took until 1841 for Whitworth to propose standard thread forms. A cheaper thread form was standardized in the United States by William Sellers in 1864 (NF, NC). The NC form was compatible with Whitworth in most sizes if you were not too fussy.

In 1948 Britain started to adopt the Unified NF and NC threads, in the middle 1960s Whitworth threads were deemed obsolete and by the late 1960s the motor industry world wide started adopting metric threads (even in the United States). As a footnote, NASA took the cheaper-to-make UNF and UNC thread form, applied the superior Whitworth technology and generated a very good but expensive hybrid.

So the message is that things start slowly and gather momentum. Even having standards does not prevent obsolescence but standards do facilitate progress.

Standardization in Our Industry

From a very early time standards have evolved from the fundamental film gauge to digital sound systems. The main body responsible for many film and TV standards is the Society of Motion Picture and Television Engineers. Although SMPTE has worldwide members, it tends to be US-centric. Relevant SMPTE standards are often put forward to International Standards institutions like the International Telecommunications Union or ISO.

In recent years there has been a shift in the ways that standards are generated. Standards often started from practical experiments, a few sales, then the need for interchangeability led to teams being set up to standardize parameters in an understandable way.

Manufacturers have become more central to the process as years go on. This can mean that marketing issues drag standards committees in one direction or another. Luckily, on balance the imposition of rigorous procedures and a healthy but possibly lengthy debate ensures that in the main no one vested interest can dominate.

The Formation of Digital Cinema Initiatives (DCI)

The digital cinema process started in a different way, with a group of people getting together to do some 'blue sky thinking' about digital cinema standards. Two years on, there was a lot of science but no practical decisions. In March 2002, seven major Hollywood studios – Paramount, Fox, Disney, Warner, Universal, Sony, MGM – keen to keep a firm hand on digital cinema, which was showing signs of developing outside of their control, formed a company called DCI or Digital Cinema Initiatives. This company was initially set up for two years to make a requirements specification for mainstream digital cinema which will cover all aspects of distribution and exhibition technology. Its mandate was extended by six months at the beginning of 2004.

Once the DCI specification (Version 3 at the time of writing) is completed to the studios' satisfaction many of its components will be put forward to the relevant standards bodies. A particular concern are the security and control systems that will be needed to keep the distributed movies safe.

There is no mandate to rubber stamp these requirements, but it is most likely that manufacturers will work together to build systems and then contribute to the standardization effort. Some of these requirements will need original R&D before it is realistic to standardize them, so we may be looking at 2006/2007 for ratified standards to the DCI requirements.

European Digital Cinema Forum (EDCF)

In Europe an association was formed in 2001 to further the spread of digital cinema. Within the EDCF are three work modules, Content, Commercial and Technical. The EDCF Commercial module generated a headline requirements document that was passed to the EDCF Technical module.

The headline requirements were as follows:

- **Better quality than 35 mm:** Better quality than 35 mm has been a common request from exhibitors, and this has led to several attempts to technically define what this means. It is certain that digital cinema systems of today can yield a quality at least as good as a commercially available release print.

As this is a new age for digital cinema, the DCI in Hollywood have suggested that any new digital cinema system should have better quality than a 35 mm studio answer print in the longer term. The EDCF would like to propose that the reference for quality be derived from camera negative, as this is then not subject to the degradations of an analogue printing process. Secondly, digital intermediate processing (see Chapter 5) is growing fast.

- **Universal system (quality tiers):** The cinema environment today varies between the headline first run blockbuster theatre with around 1500 seats to the least used screen in the multiplex, with say 150 seats. Add to this venues that may be delivering cinema to smaller communities and you realize that there have to be tiers of service.

- **Interoperability between manufacturers:** It is important for the economy of digital cinema that the system be planned with natural building blocks and that the interfaces between these blocks be standardized. For any system in the future it is desirable that there should be interoperability between the equipment from different manufacturers, thus facilitating competition, which it is hoped leads to lower cost of installation.

- **Secure and flexible transport:** Digital cinema facilitates the display of high quality studio masters anywhere in the world. Although these masters will be compressed the bit rate available will be such that they can be considered to be clones of the master files. This means that the distribution system has to be secure across any chosen transport mechanism. Transport can be via satellite, data tape, hard disc, fibre-optic etc.

- **High security system:** As mentioned above with relation to the transport, digital cinema systems have to be very secure. The security, although mostly related to the content from the point of view of direct theft, also needs to take into account unusual operational patterns within the cinema chain, for example camcorder piracy at 3.00 am! By integrating encryption systems, play list management and asset tracking, digital cinema offers better security than 35 mm. It can also be enhanced with watermarking and fingerprinting.

- **Sustainability over time:** It is important for digital cinema systems that they be built from a series of blocks that have standardized interfaces and functionality. The dilemma for the operator is obsolescence. It is not easy but it is vital to be able to upgrade systems at reasonable cost or continue to operate an existing older system.

- **Reasonable cost:** All exhibitors are concerned about the cost of investment for digital cinema. Volumes are relatively small and technology in most areas is cutting edge. This means that standardization again plays a big part. When designing systems it is important to allow them to fit within a reasonable revenue structure. It is reasonable to assume that the system designed for an auditorium of 1500 seats at a ticket price of 10 Euro will be different to that serving 150 seats at a ticket price of 6 Euro but the volume of equipment may be 10:1 or more.

Technical Levels of Service

In early EDCF Technical Module meetings during 2002 the issues of E-cinema, D-cinema, mainstream venues and community venues were discussed. (For definitions of D- and E-cinema see Chapter 1). It seemed prudent to lay out levels of service appropriate to the various venues and communities served. There are four levels suggested – Levels 4 and 3 cover E-cinema, Levels 2 and 1 cover D-cinema, 2 being current roll-out and 1 being future as standardized by SMPTE.

Level 1:   35 mm camera negative quality, circa 4K distribution resolution, wide colour gamut, file-based distribution with cinema grade security, digital cinema grade projector. Suitable for future first run theatrical release and large format presentations.

Level 2:   35 mm release print quality circa 2K distribution resolution for wide colour gamut, file-based distribution with cinema grade security, digital cinema grade projector. Suitable for mainstream first run theatrical release, may use 1.3K or 2K projection equipment.

N.B: It is recommended that Exhibitors should use equipment conforming to existing technical standards where appropriate.

Level 3:   HD quality, with HDTV resolution, HDTV colour gamut, medium security, professional grade projector. DVB distribution bit rates, second run theatrical release.

Level 4:   SDTV resolution, SDTV colour gamut, consumer level security, consumer grade projector. DVB or DVD distribution bit rates.

It is anticipated that digital cinema will reside at Level 2 for a limited time, moving on to Level 1 initially in the larger venues.

As is usual with technology, key issues catch the imagination and become highlighted without full understanding. A case in point is 2K or 4K. 2K means 2000 and is in fact 2048; 4K means 4000 and is in fact is 4096. The digital picture is made up from rows and columns of picture elements or pixels. Of course things are never as they seem: 2K in post-production is normally 2048 × 1536 – this is a Kodak norm for scanning Academy 35 mm film; 4K in post-production is normally 4096 × 3160. In digital cinema distribution these numbers are not the same: 2K means 2048 × 1080 and 4K, 4096 × 2160. This represents an aspect ratio of approximately 1.9:1, partway between 1.85:1 and 2.25:1. These aspect ratios are the finished distribution aspect ratios after post-production. A 4K picture has four times more pixels to store and transmit than a 2K picture; this means 4K systems will be significantly more expensive than 2K systems and therefore probably only be used in large cinemas initially.

10

Archiving Digital Media

Paul Read

Archivists often seem to me to treat their collection as if it were Cinderella, and they are half-way through the story. Once upon a time Cinderella was a pretty girl living her life in a dark forgotten corner. Finally the prince saw her attributes, and after a few problems and some help from her godmother, she met a prince and lived happily ever after.

What is an Archive? What is Digital Preservation?

Margaret Hedstrom, University of Michigan, Ann Arbor, defined 'digital preservation' in *Media Longevity* (National Media Lab, 1994) as:

> *The planning, resource allocation, and application of preservation methods and technologies necessary to ensure that digital information of continuing value remains accessible and usable.*

And a CLIR (Council on Library and Information Resources) publication describes digital preservation as:

> *requiring a supporting organization and infrastructure dedicated to storing the electronic files and to migrating them to new formats and/or media as technologies change. Unless these capacities are all in place, digital files cannot be regarded as permanent. Creating an enduring digital preservation master file is a multidimensional task with long-term implications.*

Image archives in this context might be defined as places in which to put images away until they are needed again, and then be able to access them easily, at both their original format, and at lower picture qualities. This definition would be accepted widely by moving image archives themselves but the definition hides an uncomfortable, and so far unattainable, objective, that applies, in particular, to film images.

Digital cinema is expected to handle similar image files (in terms of size and number) to those used for digital film restoration today and similar to those that film archives expect to preserve when film becomes unavailable, or uneconomic. Indeed most digital cinema images may well originate, at least in the first few years, from camera film originals. It is therefore relevant to review the issue of digital preservation of film images.

The FIRST Project (an Information Society Technologies (IST) EU collaborative think-tank of film archives, broadcasters and other interested parties concerned with storing film images as digital records) created a diagram to describe the inter-relationships between film, the collection and its processes (Fig. 10.1).

Original film images fade, film base decays, and every projection or viewing, or just inspection, diminishes the quality of the image usually by physical damage to the film itself. Film preservation as defined by film archivists has always been carried out by transferring the image photochemically to another film material, yet at every analogue printing process some of the original image detail and content is lost, and so the original image is inevitably degraded.

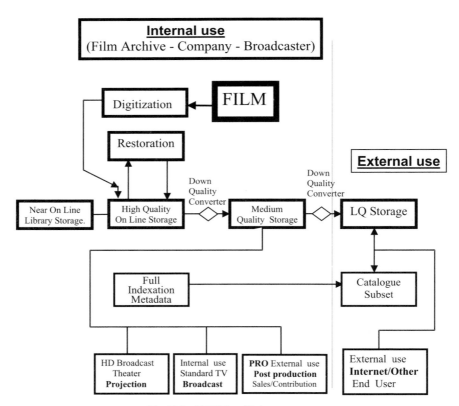

Fig 10.1   FIRST archiving strategy.

Exactly the same may be said about digitizing a film image, but in principle losses may only occur at the initial digitizing stage, as long as any subsequent duplication process, migration, is a true cloning procedure. Sadly even today we do not yet know enough about the nature of film images to be certain that our initial scanning and digitization processes are adequate to record the complete film image, but it is clear that the total film image content, at least for modern 35 mm or larger film formats, exceeds the scanning and digital media capacity we have available, or can justify.

Preservation vs. Access

Archives, in particular film archives, distinguish between preservation formats and access formats. Preservation formats are expected to retain all the image information from the original, and are, or could be, made from the image when the original is at risk from decay or image fading. Film images have far greater image content, in terms of image detail, brightness range and colour space, than any video format. 8 or 10 bit files are considered sufficient for graded final images and thus no greater bit depths will be needed for final cinema files (but 14 or 16 bit are needed for ungraded negatives, or faded film images, where grading or restoration must be done subsequently).

The following table is derived from the FIRST Project Report: State of the Art, 2003, and lists typical file sizes for current film scanning systems (which may, or may not, be the sizes chosen for the future).

Access formats are made for viewers to see the images, and vary in quality depending on the access format. In the future they will be made from the digital preservation format, the lowest quality usually being analogue VHS, and the highest a new film restoration for cinema display, made by duplication and printing, or by a high resolution digital intermediate (DI) route.

In practice all access formats today are made directly from the original film because no universally acceptable digital preservation format exists.

Archivists define the preservation format as the best image that can be obtained from the original, and the losses must be kept to a minimum. For most specialist film archives the only archival preservation image acceptable

Table 10.1 File sizes for a 90 minute, 135000 frame, 35mm feature film

Resolution	Bit depth	Capacity	Real time transfer speed
HD TV (1920 pixels × 1080 lines)	8 bit	0.56 TB	0.83 Gb/sec
2K (2048 × 1556 pixels)	10 bit	1.5 TB	2.3 Gb/sec
4K (4096 × 3112 pixels)	10 bit	6.2 TB	9.2 Gb/sec

TB = Terabytes = 10^{12} bytes
Gb/sec = Gigabits/sec = 10^9 bits/second

today is a film image made by film printing. However, in practice this is frequently a poor record of the original, or contains analogue image artefacts from the original (for example faded films may not be corrected, but simply copied in their faded state, and this is usually not correctable subsequently), or analogue image artefacts produced in the printing process.

What's the Rush?

Broadcasters have collections of both film and tape, as do archives that retain television images as well as film, and it is now quickly becoming recognized that film is less of a problem than magnetic analogue or any digital material. Film bases decay, dyes (and to some extent silver) fades, but more slowly than magnetic tape losses or decay. In addition, the effort put into research by the Image Permanence Institute and Manchester Metropolitan University over the years is paying off. It is now clear that low temperature storage can arrest both base and dye decay, extending the life of film images and optical sound, before transfer to a new base is needed. This is an economically viable alternative to the routine traditional image preservation technique of scrambling to routinely copy film to new film materials – the analogue film equivalent of digital image migration. Of course, very few film archives have so far justified this approach to their accountants and backers, in order to provide low temperature facilities, but the route and the philosophy exists. Traditional archives are also slow to use the argument that analogue film preservation copies are often poor copies of the original and lose information content and visual quality.

Parallel to improved understanding of the processes of decay is a growing realization that there is not a great rush to transfer everything to film, or digits, at once. A better approach is piecemeal as the film images and bases approach the decay that is held back by low temperature storage. The cloud on this horizon is that substantial capital sums are needed to provide these low temperature facilities. Several investigations in Europe (for example, the Danish Film Institute) have suggested that this route is less costly than the present analogue copying philosophy, or the immediate transfer and retention of digital formats. Others plan to take this route principally for nitrate film (for example, the UK Imperial War Museum).

A further cloud is the quite reasonable likelihood that film manufacture, at least of specialist duplicating films, will cease, cutting off the film preservation route, so that, for film archives, both commercial and public, the preservation of their images in a digital format becomes the only practicality.

Why Digital?

Why indeed? Digital formats, up to now, are bulky, short-lived, vulnerable to both hard and software obsolescence – analogue film has a longer life and carries a higher information density. Photographic film has been suggested as a digital information carrier, although there is little serious research on its ability. Clearly Kodachrome, and reversal monochrome films, capable of resolutions over 200 line pairs per millimetre, have possibilities. Digital technology's unique character is that when transferring, *and provided the data are cloned*, there is no loss – although therein also lies its weakness: the opportunity to compress and lose the completeness of its original information.

The plain truth is that digital technology is simply the way parallel technologies are going – cameras, broadcasting, cinemas, computers. It is inevitable and inexorable. Film will, in time, depart this world and leave it to digital media formats that cannot be held up to the light to see the picture.

The need for a digital archive format for film preservation is not limited to film archives. Broadcasters in Europe, with vast film collections, already see their collections as sources of imagery and income for the future, and since their film has far greater information density than their broadcast standard tapes, it has a wider potential range of uses, including the cinema and higher resolution television of the future. Cinema today, too, still thinks in film terms, despite, perhaps partly because, of the rising success of DI technology (see Chapter 5). This is likely to be but a passing phase – any technique that uses film in the camera, converts the analogue images to digits for post-production and then returns the image back to film is clearly a intermediate technology and may not last beyond the next generation of high resolution cameras or cinema projectors.

However, the success of the DI process (and its string of failures) should have taught us all (and I am afraid that some lessons are still being learned) that fully digital cinema, digital in the camera and digital in the projection, will need the most careful technical management and even more careful calibration. Too many current DI systems are a cobbled together miscellany of boxes, unable to display images at the intermediate post-production stages as they will be seen in the final cinema display, making grading, acceptance and signing-off an uncertain business, leading to distrust and inappropriate regrading at the final film printing stage.

These issues should be resolved before the next jump to digital production throughout – although because it is simply an intermediate process, I don't expect it will happen.

Another reason why it won't happen (my opinion, of course) is that it is becoming clear to some technologists (but with limited widespread acceptance) that it is very difficult to forecast the subjective and visual quality of a projected image from the known parameters of the component parts – resolutions, bit-depths, colour space, scanner technologies, software, hardware, compression systems, spectral range of primaries, response criteria, film recorders, digital projectors, film projectors, lights sources and visual acceptances. The film industry has known for 100 years that the best way to judge an image quality is by looking at it – the broadcast TV industry in the past admitted this only to itself, but now accepts this, especially as different TV display systems proliferate. The successful DI systems (no names … no pack drill) were calibrated using film techniques – LUTs devised to match the 'look' of an image on one display (the monitor) with the 'look' of an image on another (the cinema screen). The digital cinema industry needs to grasp this nettle now, and the Japanese Digital Cinema Consortium's experiments with varying film image sizes and different resolutions suggests this is being recognized at last.

Digital Cinema Images

And so we come to the digital cinema, and here there is clearly going to be a very different pattern of development to cinema film. In the early cinema years there were other formats than 35 mm, but very few, and none survived more than a few showings, or a few productions. Even within the 35 mm gauge, few non-standard frame dimensions succeeded that were not heavily supported by producers. Where is Cinemiracle now, or ARC120? In any case, the fundamental principles did not alter.

Digital cinema, it seems, will be different. Apart from the battling commercial technologies, there may be little appetite for real standards – where, for example, are the HD standards we all wanted? What we have instead is Table 3 of the ATSC DTV Standard, Annexe A, with over 20 possible alternative signal formats! On the other hand why should standards be set that simply restrict the progressive improvement of quality, security, simplicity and economy?

The process of digital projection is not seen as a single format for all screens. More likely are different formats for different cinemas provided some means is available to convert from the post-production format (the highest specification) to the (inevitably in some way compressed) projection format. Small cinemas may accept a projected DVD, large ones will demand 4K or more.

So we will need digital archival formats, and we will need them at the high resolution and bit depth used to make the post-production master, and because archives/producers/rights holders need to retain the maximum (or optimum) usable image information for use in future formats, some of which may be capable of greater information density than at present.

Film Images

Film images – even quite early ill-made productions on poorly manufactured film stocks – have high information densities, carry a great deal of detail, so that archivists are concerned that if and when they have to use digital preservation formats they should record all the image detail present. The problem is that there has been very little research to establish exactly what the totality of a film image is in digital terms, although both Kodak and the European Broadcasting Union have published interesting papers on the subject suggesting levels close to 4K and bit depths of 16 bit, where regrading is needed subsequently (for example for faded dyes). There are some relatively unsubstantiated demands for high resolutions and bit depths in particular: 12K pixels per horizontal line, and 20 bit has been mentioned for a 24 mm Academy frame, an impossible task today, to scan, to record onto any format, to store, or to afford. Archivists also demand that digital images from film for preservation be uncompressed, although compression is an undefined philosophy – presumably scanning a 35 mm film image at broadcast resolution and 8 bit is compression because this does not record all the information in the film image. (Note that 4K for a 35 mm Academy frame implies 2K for a 16 mm frame, and at least 8K for a 65 mm negative, and some would say 20K for a 15 perf IMAX print!)

These arguments are not purely academic, digital cinema will originate from images made from digital cameras, but also from film originals, and at this time it seems likely that the highest resolution cameras, the 4K cameras, will still be unable to equal film images in terms of the sharpness and detail. (A recent Kodak Paper suggests that a 35 mm negative film image from a 4K scanner, and then digitally enhanced, may exceed any current high resolution digital camera image.) The implication of all this is that film images will continue to be used as camera original material, at least for a while, in a digital cinema display environment, and that archival film images will continue to provide higher quality images than many or most digital cameras well into the future. Furthermore preserving digital camera images in 'lossy' compressed formats also reduces the image quality in the future below that of the original display.

Compression

There is a rising enthusiasm for heavy lossy compression to be applied to high resolution digital images (from 4K digital cameras for example simply to allow the projection at 4K or 2K at real time by today's digital projectors), and many of these images are very impressive indeed, with the temptation to compress yet further to see where the visual limit is. Necessary though this is for today's display equipment, it should have little influence on the choice of digital format for preservation, and every image should be retained at its 'natural' and camera original resolution, bit depth scale and coding. Lossless compression has been regularly considered to save 20–30% once the original scan is complete, but even these estimates are now in question. DI post-production houses using 2K and 10 bit files find that there is less than 10% to be gained by compressing film images (whose image structure is comprised of a complex grain image, in which the semi-random grain itself contributes to edge sharpness). In these circumstances even lower lossless compressions, perhaps only 5%, will be the limit for higher bit depth image files, such as 16 bit that must be used for images that require subsequent grading or image control (for example unrestored faded images).

If by now you are asking why does all this matter in choosing a digital preservation format, the answer is that the preservation master must retain all the data in the original. This is a first principle of film archive philosophy and has absolute logic for both film and video formats on its side. The EU FIRST Project (State of the Art Report, June 2003) recognizes this (even if it recognizes that in the case of film images we have no scientifically established parameters). So the next question must be, at maximum, just how much data will we need to store?

In 1990 Max Rotthaler calculated, working from published Kodak data, that a Super 35 mm colour negative film of that period should be scanned at 2950 pixels per horizontal line, and at 16 bit, making a total for a 90 minute feature of 135 000 frames of 5.5 TB. Lossless compression might reduce this to 3.5 TB. More recent information, and pragmatic viewing tests, has suggested that 4000 pixels per line at 16 bit for ungraded material, and 8–10 bit for final graded/restored material is sufficient, depending on image aspect ratios between 4 and 6 TB per feature, at the very least.

A certain well-known European commercial archive has 2000 feature film titles. That alone would require, at a minimum, 8000 TB.

The largest hard-disc-based moving image data store in Europe that I am familiar with is about 47 TB, a private company in two separate locations, used for temporary operational storage for current DI post-production and restoration. It also has its own archive of DTF tapes totalling about 25 TB, equivalent to about 100 Sony DTF tapes, but these are temporary, and as their clients 'sign off' the recorded final film negative tapes are offered to the client (who usually does not take them) or recycled.

There is obviously a disparity in what is necessary to archive digital images in quantity and what is actually possible and realistic today.

Migration

The technique originated from the fact that two different generations of drive can be installed in the same robot of an electronic library. Using dedicated software, the system is able to read old support located in one part of the library, and write onto a new support with new drive and store it in another part. This process can be fully automatic, although it often isn't, and it can work as a background or foreground task (although it often doesn't). Thus migration has come to mean any transfer of a digital file from one format/support to another.

Migration of the 8000 TB collection described above in five years time does not even bear thinking about! And this is a small film collection.

Access

Server-based systems are in use for easy access to images for TV and online access. DVD versions are now in increasingly common use for providing access to image collections. But access has been routinely confused with preservation of the image. British archivists wonder where the Viznews collection is today, and also wonder where the current British Pathé collection will be tomorrow. Both were transferred to broadcast standard access formats (Viznews more than 20 years ago, British Pathé very recently) and their film originals broken up, or passed to the dark caves of film archives, it would seem in the belief that access equals preservation.

What Should the Preservation Format Be?

So what do we need in a realistically achievable 'universal' digital archival format, whether from film or digital formats? What are the ideals?

- It should have a realistic life – an attractive proposition would be a life similar to that of fresh film, say 500 years stored below freezing, and at least 100 years in controlled climatic conditions.
- It should be scaleable and be able to handle high and low information densities (depending on the original).
- It must carry extensive metadata on a wide range of technical issues (quite apart from indexing, search and image content), including, amongst others, the software needed to open it, the display method originally used and the calibration needed to create the final displayed image.
- It must not need migration every five years. Perhaps every 50 or 100 – but not five! Few film archives and broadcasters have ever costed the digitization of their film collections for cinema purposes, let alone been able to estimate five-yearly migration costs – the current recommendation. Most film archives have nitrate material from the early twentieth century that they have not yet preserved on analogue film!

So, what suitable formats do we have available now? I will leave aside storing digital data on photographic film. None of these approaches have come to anything (although Kodak's announcement in September 2003 that it is 'changing direction', and a quiet mention of 'human readable image preservation formats' may alter that). A suggestion made within the International Federation of Film Archivists (FIAF) that they should ask a film manufacturer if the Federation could continue to run one of their film coating plants when film becomes uneconomic has, not unexpectedly, fallen on deaf ears. From most viewpoints, technical, political and economic, that would be a non-starter.

Magnetic tape systems have a high density but inherently short and troublesome lives despite some attractive costs per bit (or rather per TB). Sony's roadmap for magnetic tape suggests they can achieve increased longevity and higher recording density with their new AME technology but even so this forecast only suggests 120 Mb/sec from a single tape holding 2 TB by 2007 and still with a lifetime of only 30 years.

Hard drive magnetic systems are more immediately attractive but costly initially for large collections, and need continual maintenance. It is becoming clear that any preservation format that depends on a specialized technology just to store it, is uneconomic in space and cost.

Optical disc technology too will improve but forecasts suggest only 300 Gb by 2006.

Digital optical tape, with a capacity of 1–10 Tb/roll, transfer speeds up to 1.5 Gb/sec and a life of 100 years remain an open issue, still suggesting great promise ... but nothing more at present than a promise. And finally IBM's 'millipede' technology of minute indentations on a thin plastic film is ... also interesting.

To summarize:

Film (at 5 $^\circ$C and 35% RH)	approx. 500 years
Magnetic tape	10–50 years, eventually
Optical disc	3–200 years, with new technology
Optical tape	100+ years, but no commercial development as yet

Finally, while it is true to say that improved storage conditions for film will, or rather could, slow down the need for large quantities of images to be transferred to a digital preservation format, there are still large collections of at-risk TV formats, and it is simply impossible to estimate the costs of transferring, and subsequently migrating some of these large collections.

What is needed is a long life digital preservation format, that can sit on a shelf, costing only its space, and be ready, and easy to open, whenever it is wanted. So we will need digital archival formats ... and there isn't one.

And then there is the issue of migration – transferring the preserved images to new supports or formats to continue the life of an image.

Migration is an accountant's nightmare – despite many carefully worked out calculations the costs are always greater than anticipated, and in almost every case compromises abound – compression, 'de-accessioning' and selection are the accountant's friends.

And all the time the collection grows ... and grows.

Where Does All This Leave Us?

It seems we are left looking for a technology we don't yet have. The DI archival preservation material is still a film image (much to the relief of those Scandinavian archives who have had the greatest number of DI productions to preserve as part of their compulsory legal deposit of cinema productions). But within months this could (in Scandinavia will) change and the cinema format, in some instances, will become a set of digital files. Film producers, rights holders and collections might, probably will, have to make a new decision. Is the 'original' the uncompressed files created in the post-production house from which all the various deliverables were made – or the compressed files despatched to the cinema for projection (and there could be several versions depending on the cinema and its projection equipment).

The FIRST Project is still running, but already its conclusions are altering current attitudes to digital archiving. The project looks at moving film images which are, in general, larger than any video files and probably comparable with the anticipated digital cinema master files in the future, but increasingly its findings are resonating with all-digital moving image archiving.

These issues, listed by Eddy Goray of Radio Télévision Belge de la Communauté Française de Belgique, in the FIRST Report: State of the Art, 2003, are these:

- **Longevity:** Existing analogue films, properly stored, have a life that can be in the order of a century. Why should archivists not seek a similar longevity digital storage format? At this time, however, this is unlikely to be achieved. The best existing digital support on the market now does not have a life expectancy better than 30 years, *in the very best storage conditions.*
- **Capacity:** The most available technology on the market for storing digital is magnetic tape. This support uses the cheapest existing support technology and is able to provide the largest capacity (S-AIT format with 0.5 TeraByte (TB) in native format, and 1.3 TB using lossless compression (LLC). Unfortunately this capacity is far from able to store film or cinema images at full resolution (nominally 4K for the purposes of this explanation) using only LLC. The capacity needed could be more than 6 TB for a film of 90 minutes, requiring of five tapes of 1.3 TB each per film!

- **Speed:** The time to download or upload the digitized film to or from the digital library should not be prohibitive. Unfortunately that same 90 minute film S-AIT tape will, today, take 22 hours to upload or download one feature film!

- **Vulnerability:** Magnetic tape is sensitive to electromagnetic fields, and other supports too have short lives or very critical storage conditions for longer lives.

- **Alternative technologies:** At this time (this is the view of the FIRST team) the only other interesting and relevant storage is optical tape. Digital optical tape technology has existed since the 1980s but due to very high cost and restricted market interest there has been little commercial success. The technology has the possibility of high capacity storage in the range of 1 to 10 TB of data on one single tape unit. It is associated with high transfer rates (in the range of 0.8 to 1.5 Gb/s), although the writing process is much slower. Due to the flexible plastic used, long term storage times of more than 100 years are forecast.

- **Low life expectancy due to obsolescence:** A shorter life expectancy (even a 30 year maximum) of new digital supports creates a problem of greater impact; the consequence of rapid technological evolution changing both equipment and format more and more frequently. For the first computer generation, the life cycle was around 10 years. Now within 6 months practically each component of a computer changes, in both price and performance. The situation with software is the same, with the growing of the power of micro-processor. Software becomes more useful and more user-friendly but needs more power to run. Customers who want to use the most recent generation of software have to buy the most recent hardware.

  Analysing the roadmap of the existing different digital tape formats on the market, we can see that practically every two years the characteristics will change (in both capacity and throughput). Theoretically we have seen in the past that with each new change in support characteristics a new drive dedicated to this new support was presented. We will be obliged to change both support and drive every four, six or eight years, whether we want to or not, due to the lack of support for old equipment. The cost of such operations needs to be analysed (and often has not been considered). To add to our woes, the same can be said about the software that controls the drive.

- **Migration:** A solution to obsolescence is so-called migration. The migration process creates two main critical issues, the cost, and the duration of such a process, and both are related to the quantity of content stored in the old digital format. Careful calculation needs to be made in order to see if this kind of scenario is really manageable. We must avoid a situation where the time of migration from one format to another is bigger than the lifetime of a format, and typical cinema image files will be very large. Conceivably, migration is a policy that large cinema collections cannot justify, economically or practically, even if it is justifiable for smaller access images (and this is potentially questionable too).

Conclusion

No adequate solution exists for long term digital cinema film storage under the existing user's requirements, and increasingly it seems that this must also be said of digital cinema. It probably also applies to any large collection of image files.

- Research and development is needed on an entirely new storage support.
- Or the existing users' requirements need to be analysed and discussed with the intention to modify them in order to find a compromise that can be fulfilled by technology in the short term. If there is sufficient market potential any manufacturer will be interested (and the modern cinema film industry has similar unfulfilled requirements).
- A thorough investigation is required on the use of low levels of lossy compression to establish whether there is potential for this technology.
- Further investigation should be made of optical tape technology because this seems very well suited to the needs of large files in terms of longevity, capacity and speed. This technology seems at this time to have more benefits than other alternatives. Carefully analysed, developed, industrialized (if no drawbacks are found) and widely used (to achieve an economy of scale), this could be a possible future solution for long term digital storage.

So, Cinderella is unlikely to live happily ever after in the form in which we know her. Film and television archivists already know that their original philosophy of preserving images in their original format and support must come to an end sooner or later. Ultimately they must decide between 'content', the images and sounds, and the original technology (and of course they will choose the content). However, many of the current digital preservation policies seem just as doomed. They are, at this time, too costly, too time consuming, too inconvenient and too impermanent to be realistic.

Cinderella needs her fairy godmother.

About the Authors

Simon Bishop

Finding a reel-to-reel tape recorder under the family piano some 30 years ago began a fascination with sound recording which continues to this day. On leaving school Simon worked in the sound department for a film company making corporate films, moving on three years later to work as a freelancer. Twenty years later, and still working freelance, Simon works mostly with TV drama and feature films, though he also shoots documentaries, corporates and commercials. Recent credits include *Auf Wiedersehen Pet* for BBC1, *Life Begins* for Granada TV and some UK shooting on *Star Wars: Episode II, The Attack of the Clones.* Sb@simonbishop.com

Michael Brennan

After studying at the Royal Melbourne Institute of Technology in the degree of Illustrative Photography, Australian-born DoP Michael Brennan became the first video lighting cameraman recognized by the UK trade union. After spending 15 years shooting 120 hours of drama and documentaries on video his move into high definition was a natural progression. He was the first owner/operator of an HD camcorder in Europe and has since shot 30 HD projects, including feature films and commercials. His practical experience extends to most aspects of pre- and post-production and he is renowned for exploring both creative uses of new technology as well as integrating traditional techniques and working practices. His consultancy clients range from filmmakers, equipment manufacturers and broadcasters to software developers. Michael Brennan is Editor of *High Definition* Magazine. Vista@ntlworld.com

Richard Boyd

Richard is Head of Technical Services at the National Film Theatre (NFT) in London and Project Manager for the Digital Test Bed which is housed in the NFT. Richard has worked in the cinema exhibition industry for over 30 years, in all areas from cinema management to construction and consulting. He is currently working on the Digital Test Bed project, investigating the opportunities that digital cinema can offer for UK audiences. Richard.boyd@bfi.org.uk

Sean Foley

Sean is Raphael Nadjari's Production Designer and Post-Production Supervisor. Since 1999 they have made four feature films together: *The Shade*, presented at the Cannes Film Festival 1999 in the category *Un certain regard*; *I am Josh Polonski's Brother*, selected for the Forum at the Berlin Film Festival 2001 and distributed by MK2; *Apartment 5C*, co-produced by MK2 was selected for the 2002 Cannes Film Festival (*Quinzaine des realisateurs*); *Avanim* has recently been premiered at the 2004 Berlin Film Festival. seanfoley@bvng.com

John Graham

John joined the BBC Film Unit in Ealing Studios in 1970 as an Audio Trainee. Twenty-eight years later, in January 1998, he retired as Head of a much-changed BBC Film Unit. He then accepted the position as Director of the BKSTS, The Moving Image Society, a professional body and technical society for all those working in film, television, cinema and multimedia. During his years as the Director of the Society, BKSTS developed a significant programme of seminars and training courses in the UK, expanded its conference programme to include conferences in Europe and Asia and the now well-established BKSTS Visual Effects Conference. During this period the Society took the lead in the UK to examine and explain the new technologies associated with the development of digital cinema. In the year 2000 BKSTS got together with the UK government and colleagues in France and Sweden to initiate the European Digital Cinema Forum, which has now grown to more than 250 members across the whole of Europe. JG@wadicourt.freeserve.co.uk

Hans Hansson

Born in Karlskrona, Sweden, in 1945, Hans was educated in photography and cinematography at the Institute for Colour Photography in Lund, Sweden, 1966–70. He started a company for special effects, Technichrome in Sweden and Unichrome in London and New York, and was its Technical

Director 1980–90. Since 1980 he has been Assistant Editor for *Technology & Man Magazine*, published by the Swedish Film Institute. He teaches film and video technology at various film schools and has been DoP on many commercials, music videos, shorts and TV films. He is Vice President of the Swedish Society of Cinematographers (FSF). Hansfilm@algonet.se

Jarkko T. Laine

Born in 1969, Jarkko gained a BA in 1995 from the University of Industrial Arts (Film Department) in Helsinki. He continued his studies in London at the Royal College of Art. After an MA degree in 1997, he has worked as a freelance cinematographer, shooting TV dramas, music promos, commercials and documentaries. His feature film debut was *Elina – As if I Wasn't There* in 2003. The film has received over 20 international awards, including the Crystal Bear at Berlin Film Festival. It was also Finland's official entry to the Academy Awards (best foreign language film). Jarkko's second feature film, *Hymypoika* (Young Gods, 2003) was shot on HDCAM video. Jarkko@welho.com

Jens Ulff-Møller

Jens has a 1998 PhD in Comparative History from Brandeis University from 1998. He is the author of several articles on Danish cinema and US-European film diplomacy. His book *Hollywood's Film Wars with France: Film Trade Diplomacy and the Emergence of the French Film Quota Policy*, appeared at the University of Rochester Press in 2001. He has been Research Assistant Professor at the Department of Film Studies at the University of Copenhagen and has taught at Columbia University in the USA. Ulff@hum.ku.dk

Peter A. Packer

Following doctoral research, Peter gained an MBA with distinction and a qualification in Group Psychotherapy. He has wide experience as a CEO and consultant in cultural industries, international charities, and 'not-for-profit' organizations. Most recently he has been part of the Strategic Development Team at the UK Film Council, has facilitated cultural change in a national Scottish institution, and worked for the UK Home Office and the BBC. He has also worked with trade unions and in social exclusion projects in London and Durham. Peter has contributed widely to film culture in the UK – publishing and broadcasting on Spanish cinema, being founder and creative director of the Lesbian and Gay Film Festival (now an annual event at The National Film Theatre in London). In January 2004 he organized 'Inform and Empower: Media Literacy in the 21st Century', a groundbreaking seminar for the film and television industry, government and education agencies on behalf of the UK Film Council, the British Film Institute, Channel 4 and the BBC. Peter.packer@ukfilmcouncil.org.uk

Paul Read

Born in 1938, Paul studied chemistry, biology and mathematics at University College, London. He joined Kodak Ltd Research, later managing an international Kodak motion picture training school in the UK and the USA. He was director of a London film lab in the 1970s and has been an independent consultant on technical management, digital and film post-production and restoration since 1979 with clients throughout the world. They recently include Soho Images, Digital Film Lab, facility and laboratory companies, rights holders and collections, insurance companies and the courts. He is currently consultant to the EU FIRST project (Film Restoration & Conservation Strategies), a member of the Technical Commission of FIAF and an EBU film scanning group. He has written several books and numerous papers. He lectures on digital technology for modern film post-production and archive film restoration for archive and Media Masters degrees at several European and American universities. ReadHF@aol.com

Kees Ryninks

Between 1977 and 1981 Kees was a student in direction and production at the National Film School in Beaconsfield, England, having worked in the Dutch film industry as a sound recordist since the age of 19. Following his graduation he worked as a cameraman and independent producer and director for BBC, Channel Four and ITV, amongst others. Since 1993 he has produced more than 20 (theatre) documentaries, six of them winning major awards in Europe and the USA. In 1997 he founded Ryninks Films and moved back to Amsterdam. Since January 2001 he has been Head of Documentaries at the Netherlands Film Fund (NFL), with the specific task of reorganizing the Dutch documentary sector. In February 2002 he initiated DocuZone, a concept in which ten film theatres are being equipped with state-of-the-art digital equipment for showing two documentaries each month. Presently he is spearheading the European DocuZone initiative in which eight countries collaborate in setting up a digital documentary network across Europe, suitable for specialized feature films, documentaries, shorts and animation. k.ryninks@filmfund.nl

Steve Shaw

Through Digital Praxis Steve provides front-line support for companies operating in the high technology arena of digital imaging within the creative film and video image market place. Steve is both a technologist, involved in building digital intermediate business operations, as well as an experienced hands-on creative. He has credits on numerous films and commercials, from *Elizabeth* to *Piazza Delle Cinque Lune*, for various roles performed. Previously he has been Technical Director at Cintel International Ltd, MD of Postware Ltd (a sister company to Cintel), MD of Men in White Coats Ltd (a digital visual effects company in Soho, London) and Marketing Manager at Quantel Ltd, specializing in high-end video and film projects. Steve@digitalpraxis.net

Roland Sterner

Roland was born in 1943 and studied still photography and documentary film for Christer Strömholm 1965–67. He worked as assistant cameraman on feature film productions 1968–79 and made several documentaries, shorts and commercials as cinematographer. His debut as Director of Photography was *Children's Island* (*Barnens ö*) in 1979, with several features following as DoP 1980–85. He worked at the Swedish Film Institute, Department of Technical Information 1985–88 and started a career as film educator during that time. From 1996 he was Cinematography Teacher at Dramatiska Institutet, the Swedish University College for Film, Radio, Television and Theatre. roland.sterner@draminst.se

Lasse Svanberg (Editor)

Born in Kalix, Sweden, in 1937, Lasse studied at the Royal School of Arts, Crafts & Design (Stockholm) 1958–60, Institute of Design (Chicago) 1961–62 and the Swedish Film School (Cinematography Department) 1964–66. He was Director of Photography on 14 feature films between 1966 and 1981. He founded *Technology & Man Magazine* (*Tidskriften TM*) at the Swedish Film Institute 1968 and was its Chief Editor until 1998 and is the author of six books on the history and development of moving images, the latest being *TV Images – 50 Years of Swedish TV Production History* published by SVT/SR (2001). He was elected Fellow of the British Kinematograph Sound and Television Society (BKSTS) 1979 and Fellow of the Society of Motion Picture and Television Engineers (SMPTE) 1995. He was one of the founders of the EDCF Content Module and member of the

Steering Committee of EDCF since 2001. In August 2002 he was granted the title of Professor by the Swedish government (Ministry of Culture). He retired from the Swedish Film Institute in 2003 and now runs a small consultancy firm of his own as speaker and writer. Lasse.svanberg@chello.se

Patrick von Sychowski

Patrick is Senior Analyst for London-based media research company Screen Digest (www.screendigest.com). He is the author of 'Electronic Cinema: the Big Screen Goes Digital', the first report ever published on the subject of digital distribution and exhibition of film and alternative entertainment. Patrick is the founder and editor of the weekly industrial e-mail newsletter *The E-Cinema Alert*, with over 1500 subscribers across the world. He has acted as adviser to several European government digital initiatives, including being a founding member of the European Digital Cinema Forum (EDCF). A frequent speaker and lecturer at international cinema and film events, Patrick was most recently involved in the setting up of a UK/European Digital Test Bed in London, as well as advising the UK Film Council in its Digital Screen Network project to digitalize a quarter of all cinemas in the UK by the end of 2004. Patrick.vonsychowski@screendigest.com

Sarah Trigg

Sarah is administrator for the Digital Test Bed project at the National Film Theatre and works with Richard Boyd on setting up the various event and seminars. She has worked at the Technical Department of NFT for seven years and has just completed her MA Degree in Arts Management, specializing in digital cinema exhibition and its implications for the UK film industry. Sarah.trigg@bifi.org.uk

Peter Wilson

Born in 1952, Peter left school at 15 to enter the electronics industry via an apprenticeship. Most of the 1970s were spent in Portsmouth Polytechnic in Electrical Engineering and TV studios. In 1978 he moved to the Royal College of Art's Film & TV school as studio engineer, in 1979 he moved to the National Film & TV School and then in 1981 to Sony Broadcast, starting in HDTV 1985 and ultimately running the Sony HDTV business in Europe. This included supporting RAI with the production of *Julia & Julia*. He organized the first-ever transmission of large screen pictures into a commercial cinema in conjunction with BT (1988, 1125 GBps via fibre). He moved to Snell & Wilcox in 1991, initially spearheading HD and Display Processing Business, latterly concentrating on digital cinema. He was the founding chair of the EDCF Technical Module in 2001. Peter.wilson@snellwilcox.com

Further Reading

Books, Magazines and Specific Articles

Being Digital by Nicholas Negroponte (Alfred A. Knopf, New York 1995). A thought-provoking, technosophical introduction to the digital world by the founder of MIT Media Lab.

Electronic Cinematography – Achieving Photographic Control over the Video Image by Harry Mathias and Richard Patterson (Wadsworth Publishing Company, USA 1985). A 'classic' in the sense that it was the first book of its kind, mapping out the interfaces between cinematography and video in the Pre-Digital Age.

Digital Filmmaking – The Changing Art and Craft of Making Motion Pictures by Thomas A. Ohanian and Michael E. Phillips (Focal Press, 2000, 2nd edition including 24p and HDTV). Gives a broad perspective on how the digital development affects various parts of the filmmaking process. By the same authors, *The 24p Format – The Universal Mastering Format* (Focal Press, 2003 including CD and website www.24p.com).

Definition – The HiDef Source Book 2003.5 (OZ Publishing, USA, 2003). A production directory on HD crew, equipment, production (80 specific categories) and post-production resources. Can be accessed online or bought (50 USD) at www.ozonline.tv.

High Definition and 24p Cinematography by Paul Wheeler (Focal Press, 2003). A recent and therefore very useful 'how-to-do-it' book on the practicalities of HD cinematography, from pre-production and choice of HD cameras to crewing and post-production. By the same author, *Digital Cinematography* (Focal Press, 2001).

American Cinematographer. The official journal of American Society of Cinematographers (85 years old in 2004) and the biggest international trade magazine dealing specifically (and monthly) with the art and craft of cinematography. www.theasc.com

High Definition Magazine – The Magazine for HD, 2K and Beyond. An exclusive magazine (published in the UK) on the latest in HD production, with tech-news, statistics and well-illustrated articles. Subs@definitionmagazine.com. www.definitionmagazine.com.

Image Technology. The journal of BKSTS, The Moving Image Society. Covers all sides of moving image production (plus special issues on cinema technology). Free for BKSTS members, for subscription contact wendy@bksts.com. www.bksts.com

The E-Cinema Alert Newsletter. A bi-weekly electronic newsletter, free of charge, edited by Patrick von Sychowski, Senior Analyst at Screen Digest, London. Gives an updated international perspective on the development of E- and D-cinema on all levels. www.screendigest.com

'The Death of Film/The Decay of Cinema' by Godfrey Cheshire (*New York Press*, Volume 12, issue 34). http://www.nypress.com/col 1.cfm?content_id=243.

'A Digital Cinema of the Mind? Could Be' by Walter Murch (*New York Times* 2 May 1999). http://faculty.marymt.edu/hopper/TMMU201/digimind.html.

The Hollywood Reporter 'Digital Cinema White Paper 2003'. http://www. hollywoodreporter.com/thr/film/feature_display,jsp?vnu_content_id=1987713

Websites

www.edcf.net
European Digital Cinema Forum (EDCF) informs about meetings, seminars and current projects by the Technical Module, the Commercial Module and the Content Module.

www.dtvprofessional.com
News and technical articles on digital TV and HDTV.

http://hd24.com
British DoP Michael Brennan's website where he generously shares his vast HD experience with others.

www.cinematography.net
British DoP Geoff Boyle has initiated an interesting international discussion forum (Cinematography Mailing List) on the pros and cons of the transition to digital. In addition the site contains very useful technical information and reports on tests.

www.sonyuscinealta.com
Sony USA's site for news, articles on current HD productions and products.

www.cinealta.com   www.sonybiz.net/HDCAM
As the above, but on a more international level.

www.sony.com/DMP
Digital Motion Pictures

www.apple.com/finalcutpro/hd.html
News about Final Cut Pro and cost-effective HD editing.

www.panasonic.com/PBDS/subcat/Products/cams_ccorders/f_aj-hdc27v.html
A long address to Panasonic's own website on DVC PRO-HD, Varicam Cinema and 720p HD.

http://jkor.com/peter/contentshd.html
DoP Peter Gray's site with several interesting pages on HD production, menu settings and film vs. video discussions.

www.DigitalCinemaSolutions.org
Guiding you along the Digital Frontier. A site initiated by among others DoP James Mathers, Migrant FilmWorkers and Brian McKernan, Digital Cinema Magazine, developing a new independent society, The Digital Cinema Society.

www.cameraguild.com/technology/index.htm
A 'gold mine' in terms of interesting articles and papers (new and old) on the transition from analogue to digital techniques within the professional film industry.

www.88824pfilm.com
The site of VideoShots.nets and DoP Ken Garff containing advice and articles on HD production (among others Robert Rodriguez' 'Digital Desperado').

http://entertainment.howstuffworks.com/hdtv.htm
A consumer-oriented site on how HDTV, MPEG 2 compression etc. works, well worth reading also for film pros.

www.film-and-video.com/HDmonitorsetup.html#colorbars
Useful advice on how HD monitors should be set up and calibrated.

http://videoexpert.home.att.net/artic3/
A site where, among others, spreadsheets of comparisons between different HD recording formats can be found.

www.2-pophd.com
One of Creative Planet's sites containing HD technical news and articles. Other useful CPC sites are *www.uemedia.net/CPC/digitalcinemamag* (Digital Cinema Magazine) and *www.cinematographer.com.*

www.bfi.org.uk/features/dtb/
The NFT Digital Test Bed.

www.dlp.com
Texas Instrument's DLP Cinema site.

www.digitalcinemareport.com
US news source for wide screen production and presentation.

www.thomsongrassvalley.com/viper
News on the Viper FilmStream camera.

www.dalsa.com
News on the Canadian DALSA camera, click on Digital Cinema.

www.dcinematoday.com
Digital Cinema Today.

www.cst.fr
Commission Supérieure Technique del'Image et du Son (CST) is a standard-setting French government body (part of CNC), doing advanced research in cinema, projector and camera technology. The site also contains their newsletter, *La Lettre de la CST*.

www.smpte.org
US-based Society of Motion Picture and Television Engineers (SMPTE) – setting the standard in motion imaging – publishes monthly *SMPTE Motion Imaging Journal*, has numerous work groups and committees. Work Group DC.28 (with seven sub-groups) deals with the development of an international digital cinema standard.

Index